W9-AQP-484

THE GREAT ADVENTURE

From a photograph, copyright by Pirie MacDonald

THEODORE ROOSEVELT

THE
GREAT ADVENTURE

PRESENT–DAY STUDIES IN
AMERICAN NATIONALISM

BY
THEODORE ROOSEVELT

NEW YORK
CHARLES SCRIBNER'S SONS
1918

TO
**ALL WHO IN THIS WAR HAVE PAID WITH
THEIR BODIES FOR THEIR SOULS' DESIRE**

FOREWORD

WE should accept from Germany what our allies have wrung from Austria and Turkey— unconditional surrender. This ought to be our war aim; and until this war aim is achieved the peace terms should be discussed only with our allies and not with our enemies. In broad outline, it is possible now to state what these peace terms should include: Restitution by Germany of what she has taken and atonement for the wrong she has done; her complete military withdrawal from every foot of territory outside her own limits; and the giving not of "autonomy"—a slippery word used by slippery people to mean anything or nothing—but of complete independence to the races subject to the dominion of Germany, Austria, and Turkey (which means the creation of the free commonwealths of the Poles, Czecho-Slovaks, and Armenians, and therefore the expulsion of the Turk from Europe), the absolute freeing of Russia from the German stranglehold, and aid generously furnished by us to Russia, the retention

by England and Japan of the colonies they have
conquered, the restoration and indemnification
of Belgium, the return of Alsace-Lorraine to
France, the creating of a Jugo-Slav commonwealth, the joining to Italy of Italian Austria
and to Roumania of Roumanian Hungary.

When the manuscript of this volume was
turned in, and even up to the time of the revi-
sion of the last galley-proofs, it seemed that,
as regards the major part of what is above set
forth, I was taking substantially the position
to which, after much hesitation, much indeci-
sion, and much talking every which way, the
administration was tending steadily to come.
Apparently our government intended to fight
the war through to the peace of overwhelming
victory. Then, without warning, and apparently
without consultation with our allies, the President entered into a correspondence or negotia-
tion about peace terms with Germany, which
looked as if we had gotten back to the bad old
days when note-writing and conversation were
considered by Mr. Wilson as adroit and sufficient answers to the sinking of the *Lusitania*
and similar German crimes. It was the attitude of an untrustworthy friend and an irreso-

lute foe, and if accepted by the nation would have caused our people to forfeit their own self-respect and the respect of all other nations. However, the outburst of protest against the President's action was such that he promptly reversed himself again, and after having invited Germany's offer, repudiated it with indignation. We all trust that he will persevere in this attitude; but we do not profess any certainty of conviction in the matter.

The Germans, while they are conducting their military retreat with formidable efficiency, are carrying on an adroit peace offensive, designed to save Germany from wreck and leave her an unpunished menace to the future of the world. They hope to succeed by appealing to those leaders of the Allies (especially in the United States) who are infirm of purpose and wavering of will.

What is needed at this time is not the compounding of felony by the discussion of terms with the felons, but the concentration and speedy development of our whole strength so as to overwhelm Germany in battle and to dictate to her the peace of unconditional surrender.

Moreover, our people ought emphatically to repudiate the "fourteen points" offered by President Wilson as a satisfactory basis for peace. We ought likewise to repudiate all of his *similar* proposals (some of his utterances have been satisfactory, but all of these have been contradicted by his other utterances, and no one can be sure which set of utterances will receive his ultimate adherence). Some of these fourteen points are mischievous under any interpretation. Most of them are worded in language so vague and so purely rhetorical that they may be construed with equal justice as having diametrically opposite meanings. Germany and Austria have eagerly approved these fourteen points; our own pro-Germans, pacifists, socialists, anarchists, and professional internationalists also approve them; but good citizens, who are also sound American nationalists, will insist upon all of them being put into straightforward and definite language— and then will reject most of them.

Under these conditions I do not know what action our government may now be secretly planning or what course it will follow even in the immediate future. But no matter what

this action may be, the course of conduct advocated in this volume is in my judgment the
only course that can with honor and safety be
followed by the American people.   Our present
business is to fight, and to continue fighting
until Germany is brought to her knees.   Our
next business will be to help guarantee the
peace of justice for the world at large, and to
set in order the affairs of our own household.

THEODORE ROOSEVELT.

SAGAMORE HILL; November 6, 1918.

CONTENTS

CONTENTS

THE GREAT ADVENTURE

CHAPTER I

THE GREAT ADVENTURE

ONLY those are fit to live who do not fear to die; and none are fit to die who have shrunk from the joy of life and the duty of life. Both life and death are parts of the same Great Adventure. Never yet was worthy adventure worthily carried through by the man who put his personal safety first. Never yet was a country worth living in unless its sons and daughters were of that stern stuff which bade them die for it at need; and never yet was a country worth dying for unless its sons and daughters thought of life not as something concerned only with the selfish evanescence of the individual, but as a link in the great chain of creation and causation, so that each person is seen in his true relations as an essential part of the whole, whose life must be made to serve the larger and continuing life of the whole. Therefore it is that the man who is not willing to die, and the woman who is not willing to send her man to die, in a war for a great cause, are not worthy to live. Therefore it is that the man and woman who in peace-time fear or ignore the primary and vital duties and the high happiness of family life, who dare not beget and bear and rear the life that is to last when they are in their graves, have broken the chain of creation, and have shown that they are unfit for companionship with the souls ready for the Great Adventure.

The wife of a fighting soldier at the front recently wrote as follows to the mother of a gallant boy, who at the front had fought in high air like an eagle, and, like an eagle, fighting had died:

I write these few lines—not of condolence for who would dare to pity you?—but of deepest sympathy to you and yours as you stand in the shadow which is the earthly side of those clouds of glory in which your son's life has just passed. Many will envy you that when the call to sacrifice came you were not found among the paupers to whom no gift of life worth offering had been entrusted. They are the ones to be pitied, not we whose dearest are jeoparding their lives unto the death in the high places of the field. I hope my two sons will live as worthily and die as greatly as yours.

There spoke one dauntless soul to another!
America is safe while her daughters are of this
kind; for their lovers and their sons cannot
fail, as long as beside the hearthstones stand
such wives and mothers. And we have many,
many such women; and their men are like
unto them.

With all my heart I believe in the joy of
living; but those who achieve it do not seek
it as an end in itself, but as a seized and prized
incident of hard work well done and of risk
and danger never wantonly courted, but never
shirked when duty commands that they be
faced. And those who have earned joy, but
are rewarded only with sorrow, must learn
the stern comfort dear to great souls, the comfort that springs from the knowledge taught
in times of iron that the law of worthy living
is not fulfilled by pleasure, but by service,
and by sacrifice when only thereby can service
be rendered.

No nation can be great unless its sons and
daughters have in them the quality to rise
level to the needs of heroic days. Yet this
heroic quality is but the apex of a pyramid of
which the broad foundations must solidly rest

on the performance of duties so ordinary that to impatient minds they seem commonplace. No army was ever great unless its soldiers possessed the fighting edge. But the finest natural fighting edge is utterly useless unless the soldiers and the junior officers have been through months, and the officers of higher command and the general staff through years, of hard, weary, intensive training. So likewise the citizenship of any country is worthless unless in a crisis it shows the spirit of the two million Americans who in this mighty war have eagerly come forward to serve under the Banner of the Stars, afloat and ashore, and of the other millions who would now be beside them overseas if the chance had been given them; and yet such spirit will in the long run avail nothing unless in the years of peace the average man and average woman of the duty-performing type realize that the highest of all duties, the one essential duty, is the duty of perpetuating the family life, based on the mutual love and respect of the one man and the one woman, and on their purpose to rear the healthy and fine-souled children whose coming into life means that the family and, therefore, the nation shall continue in life and shall not end in a sterile death.

Woe to those who invite a sterile death; a death not for them only, but for the race; the death which is insured by a life of sterile selfishness.

But honor, highest honor, to those who fearlessly face death for a good cause; no life is so honorable or so fruitful as such a death. Unless men are willing to fight and die for great ideals, including love of country, ideals will vanish, and the world will become one huge sty of materialism. And unless the women of ideals bring forth the men who are ready thus to live and die, the world of the future will be filled by the spawn of the unfit. Alone of human beings the good and wise mother stands on a plane of equal honor with the bravest soldier; for she has gladly gone down to the brink of the chasm of darkness to bring back the children in whose hands rests the future of the years. But the mother, and far more the father, who flinch from the vital task earn the scorn visited on the soldier who flinches in battle. And the nation should by action mark its attitude alike toward the fighter in war and toward the child-bearer in peace and war. The vital need of the nation is that its men and women of the future shall be the sons and daughters of the soldiers of the present. Excuse no man from going to war because he is married; but put all unmarried men above a fixed age at the hardest and most dangerous tasks; and provide amply for the children of soldiers, so as to give their wives the assurance of material safety.

In such a matter one can only speak in general terms. At this moment there are hundreds of thousands of gallant men eating out their hearts because the privilege of facing death in battle is denied them. So there are innumerable women and men whose undeserved misfortune it is that they have no children or but one child. These soldiers denied the perilous honor they seek, these men and women heart-hungry for the children of their longing dreams, are as worthy of honor as the men who are warriors in fact, as the women whose children are of flesh and blood. If the only son who is killed at the front has no brother because his parents coldly dreaded to play their part in the Great Adventure of Life, then our sorrow is not for them, but solely for the son who himself dared the Great Adventure of Death. If, however, he is the only son because the Unseen Powers denied others to the love of his father and mother, then we mourn doubly with them because their darling went up to the sword of Azrael, because he drank the dark drink proffered by the Death Angel.

In America to-day all our people are summoned to service and sacrifice. Pride is the portion only of those who know bitter sorrow or the foreboding of bitter sorrow. But all of us who give service, and stand ready for sacrifice, are the torch-bearers. We run with the torches until we fall, content if we can then pass them to the hands of other runners. The torches whose flame is brightest are borne by the gallant men at the front, and by the gallant women whose husbands and lovers, whose sons and brothers are at the front. These men are high of soul, as they face their fate on the shell-shattered earth, or in the skies above or in the waters beneath; and no less high of soul are the women with torn hearts and shining eyes; the girls whose boy lovers have been struck down in their golden morning,

and the mothers and wives to whom word has
been brought that henceforth they must walk
in the shadow.

These are the torch-bearers; these are they
who have dared the Great Adventure.

CHAPTER II

THE MEN WHO PAY WITH THEIR BODIES FOR THEIR SOULS' DESIRE

IN a great war for the right the one great debt owed by the nation is that to the men who go to the front and pay with their bodies for the faith that is in them. At the front there are of course of necessity a few men who, from the nature of the case, are not in positions of great danger—as regards the staff and the high command, the burden of crushing responsibility borne by such men outweighs danger. But as a rule the men who do the great work for the nation are the men who, for a money payment infinitely less than what they would earn in civil life, face terrible risk and endure indescribable hardship and fatigue and misery at the front. These men include the air fighters, who run the greatest risk of all; and the fighting foot-sluggers, the infantry,—the "doughboys,—" and the marines,

9

and the machine-gun men, who take the terrible punishment when the tremendous thrusts are made; and the engineers and the men in the tanks and the men with the field-guns and the heavier guns, and the men who manage the gas—the work of all of whom is absolutely indispensable and who do it in hourly peril of their lives; and the doctors and stretcher-bearers who suffer the same dangers as the men to whom they bring succor; and the men who bring up the munition-trains—in short, all who under fire join in the exhausting and perilous labor which brings victory. These are the real heroes. These are the men who do the one great and indispensable task which entitles them forever to be honored by all true Americans.

The rest of us behind the lines are merely supplementing their work. I have no patience with the well-meaning, silly persons who now and then announce that "saving will win the war" or that "money will win the war" or that "food will win the war." Let these good persons speak the truth and say that Liberty Bonds and Thrift Savings Stamps and the production of food and munitions and the practice of economy and the work done through organizations like the Red Cross will all help to win the war and are indispensable. But the war will be won by the fighting men at the front! Every other activity in this nation is merely auxiliary to theirs.

From General Pershing down the men of our army overseas have won for themselves deathless fame and have reflected the highest honor upon this nation. I know personally of division, brigade, and regimental commanders who, in addition to high valor, have shown an efficiency which puts them on a level with the very best men of their rank in any service in the world—I do not mention their names, merely because to do so would probably do an injustice to others equally good about whom I do not know. As for the battalion and company and platoon officers and non-commissioned officers and rank and file, I do not think it is untruthful or exaggerated to say that on the whole when our troops have finished their training they stand a little above the average of any other army in the world to-day. The seven or eight American divisions who did the murderous fighting in July and August during Foch's great counter-offensive established a record such as only the few very finest troops of any other army could equal, and which could not be surpassed. Probably in our own history nothing has ever quite come up to it, save in certain actions during the Civil War. The endurance, the valor, the efficiency, the fighting edge of these men could not be surpassed. Their losses correspond to their achievements. (In the infantry regiment in which two of my sons served, the colonel, the lieutenant-colonel, the three majors, and almost all the captains and lieutenants were killed or wounded; and the loss was proportionally almost as great among the enlisted men.) In addition to these divisions there were two or three times as many other divisions, across the seas or about to cross the seas, who were composed of as fine fighting material, and who by this time are probably as efficient, but who had not at that period been sufficiently trained to do the heaviest assault work. But they have been trained now; Pershing's army began its great thrust, as a separate army, about a year and a half after we entered the war. The actual management of our oversea army work is now excellent; and the quality of our troops is really extraordinary.

The noted French sociologist Gustave Le Bon writes me:

My compatriots have discovered an America of which they had no idea. In addition to the heroism of her soldiers she has revealed aptitudes for scientific method and organization, the fruits of her education, which have awakened our admiration. Harbors, railroads, factories rise as if by magic. Every one asks how such men were trained and instructed.

Our men include Americans from every section of the country and from every walk of life. The son of the railroad president and the son of the brakeman, the college graduate and the man who left a plough-tail at the end of the furrow, or threw down his pick and shovel or his ax and saw, all stand on the same plane, and do the same work and face and meet the same dangers. The son of the wealthy man who has been reared softly, and the son of the man who has every day eaten his bread in the sweat of his brow, look death in the eyes with the same stern courage and do their hard grinding work with the same grim efficiency. In the intervals of work they are light-hearted and they enjoy themselves greatly, snatching the pleasures with an added zest, because peril is so very near. Protestant and Catholic, Jew and Gentile, men of old native American stock, and men whose parents were born abroad or who themselves were born abroad—no distinction whatever can be made among them as they do their allotted tasks.

The moods in which they have accomplished these tasks vary as widely as the tasks themselves. But the work is well done, whether inspired by matter-of-fact acceptance of the fact that the United States is at war and that therefore it is up to the men of fighting age to do the fighting men's job; or by the exalted idealism of the young Galahad whose eyes are open to the shining visions shrouded from duller sight—and the young Galahads of this great war when they have found the grail have too often filled it with their own hearts' blood.

Some have been driven by a sense of duty to do the best there was in them in a task for which they have no natural desire. Others eagerly welcome the chance to sweep straight as a falcon at the quarry which may be death; and these may come back with broken wings; or they may never come back, and word may be brought to the women who weep that they must walk henceforth in the shadow. But all alike have done their duty and more than their duty; and their souls shall stand forever in the glory of the morning; and all who dwell in this land now, or who shall dwell in it in the future, owe to them a debt that can never be cancelled.

And the first instalment of payment on this debt should be paid by the government to the wives and children and dependent mothers left by the man who goes to the front. The wife who cheers him when he goes, and the children whom he leaves behind when he goes, should be amply provided for as a matter of mere justice. I believe that the state should in some way endow motherhood anyhow; but there can be no question of our duty toward the mother of the children whose father has left her and them to go to war.

We are fighting for our dearest rights. We are also fighting for the rights of all peoples, small or great, so long as they are well-behaved and do not wrong others, to enjoy their liberty and govern themselves in the forms they see fit to adopt. We intend to try to help others, but we know well that we cannot do so unless we are able to do justice within our own borders, and to manage well the affairs of our own household. Therefore it behooves us, even now while we are bending all our energies to winning the great war, also to look to the future, and to begin to ponder the things that we must do to bring greater happiness and well-being and a higher standard of conduct and character within our own borders when once the war is through.

Surely all of us—and especially those of us who stay at home and who are denied the opportunity to go to the front—ought to realize the need in this country of a loftier idealism than we have had in the past; and the further and even greater need that we should in actual practice live up to the ideals we profess. The things of the body have a rightful place and a great place. But the things of the soul should have an even greater place. There has been in the past in this country far too much of

that gross materialism which, in the end, eats
like an acid into all the finer qualities of our
souls.

The war came—our gross ideals were shattered and the scales fell from our eyes, and we
saw things as they really were. Suddenly in
the awful presence of death we grew to understand the true values of life. We realized
that only those men were fit to live who were
not afraid to die; that although death was a
terrible thing, yet that there were other things
that were more terrible, other things that made
life not worth living. All the finest of our
young men, all those high of soul, responded
eagerly to the call to arms; the son of the rich
man and the son of the poor man, side by side,
neither claiming any favor except the chance
to win honor and perform duty in the face of
deadly peril. These men who have been going,
and are going abroad by the million, are sacri-
ficing everything for the sake of a great ideal.
They have shown their willingness to sacrifice
money and ease and pleasure, and life itself
when duty calls, and the nation bids them go.
Let us who are left behind in our turn strive to
make our lives a little nearer the right ideal.

Let us introduce into the work of peace something of the spirit that they have introduced into the work of war. When these men come home, or at least when those of them who escape death come home, I believe that they will demand, and I know that they ought to demand, a juster type of life, socially and industrially, in this country. I believe, and I hope, that they will demand a loftier idealism in both our public and private affairs, and better and more common-sense methods of reducing our ideals to practice and making them realizable. I believe that they will themselves show both idealism and also that common sense the lack of which insures disaster in peace as in war. I think they will insist upon a livelier sense of brotherhood and yet will no less insist upon the duty of recognizing leadership. Our aim must be to raise the level of the table-land of general opportunity and welfare without lowering the peaks of high achievement. Let the difference of reward be as great as that between our generals and admirals, such as Pershing and Sims, and the warrant officers or senior non-commissioned officers under them. But let there be a better proportion than is now the case in industrial life, between the service rendered and the reward given. Gradually I hope to see the wage-worker become in a real sense a partner in the enterprise in which he works; and to achieve this end he must develop the power of self-control, the power of recognizing the rights of others no less than insisting upon his own; he must develop common sense; and that strength of character which cannot be conferred from without, and the lack of which renders everything else of no avail. Above all, I wish to see the farmers develop their strength by co-operation and in other ways, so that the elemental work of the soil will resume its ancient importance among us.

At this moment we can only lay the foundation in outline; but there are certain things that we should do at once in connection with the war. One of them is to stop all profiteering by capitalists; and another is to stop all slacking and loafing, whether by undividual workmen or as a result of union action. Of these two perhaps the profiteer is worse; but the slacker is almost as bad. As for the profiteer, any man who makes a fortune out of this war ought to be held up to derision and scorn. No man should come out of this war materially ahead of what he was when we went into it. There must be the reward for capital necessary in order to make it profitable to do the necessary work, and to cover the necessary risks; this is indispensable, and the government should see that neither demagogy nor ignorance interferes with this necessary reward. But we heartily approve, as a war measure, of heavy progressive taxation of all profits, beyond the reasonable profits necessary for the continuance of industry, and our governmental authorities would do well to see whether it is not possible to put a tax on unused land. Most of our captains of finance are doing with all their energy necessary governmental work without any financial reward for themselves. I honor these men, I honor their sons who have gone to the war. But I have scant patience with the other men who treat the war merely as a chance for profit; and I have least patience with the rich men who keep their sons at home. I will not excuse the poor man from going to war; but I would make it obligatory on the man who has much. As for the profiteer, if I could get at him I would like to put him to digging the front trenches. And I would put beside him his brother in wrong-doing, the slacker or loafer, the man who limits the output, when it is necessary at this time that we should have the greatest possible production; and I would do this whether he was acting as an individual, or as an official or member of a labor union. Pershing's men are not limiting their output, and shame and disgrace should be the portion of any man who limits his output here at home.

I believe that when this war is over we should prepare for our self-defense against other nations, and I believe that we should prepare for our own inner development. And in order to meet both needs, I believe in the principle of universal service. Of this military service is but a part. It is a vital part, and under no circumstances can we neglect it. But it is only a part. Universal suffrage can be justified only by universal service, service in peace and service in war. The man who will not render this service has no right to the vote. If he won't fight for the country in war and do his duty by the country in peace, we ought not to permit him to vote in the country. The conscientious objector who won't serve as a soldier or won't pay his taxes has no place in a republic like ours, and should be expelled from it, for no man who won't pull his weight in the boat has a right in the boat. The Society of Friends have come forward in this war just as gallantly as they came forward in the Civil War, and all true believers in peace will do well to follow their example.

We now have an approach to the universal service which some of us have for many years been demanding. We now have all men from eighteen to forty-five required to serve their country, and required to register. Let us make this system permanent, and let us use it for the purposes of peace no less than for the purposes of war. Let us extend the principle to women no less than to men. Let us base suffrage on service. Let us demand the service from women as we do from men, and in return give the suffrage to all men and women who, in peace and war perform the service, and to no others. Base suffrage on service and not on sex. Treat it not as an unearned privilege but as a duty which each of us

is to perform in a spirit of service to all of us
and as a right which is not to be enjoyed unless the person enjoying it does his or her full
duty in peace and war.

Universal training is a prerequisite for efficient universal service. It is just as much a
prerequisite for efficient service in war as for
efficient service in peace. It is just as much a
prerequisite for women as for men. At this
moment we have embodied in law the principle
of universal military service for men, but inasmuch as there has never been universal obligatory military training for the service, we now
have to do all this training during the war itself. In consequence we were not able to exert
any considerable fraction of our man-power
until over a year after we went to war; and
over two years will have elapsed before the
proportion of our strength thus actually usable
and used will be anywhere near as great as the
proportion of the French, English, or Italian
strength thus used. This means that during
the first year of the war we would have been
absolutely helpless, and during the first year
and a half almost helpless, against our antago-
nists if we had not been protected by the

armies and navies of our allies. In other
words, while we were hardening our unprepared and helpless strength, and making it
ready, we were saved from the strength and
fury of our enemy only by the strength and
valor of our allies. We now have universal
military service. If four years ago we had had
universal military training, so that the service
would have been immediately efficient when
called for, the war would have been over within
ninety days from the time we entered it, and
infinite bloodshed and treasure would have
been spared. Next time we may not have
allies to protect us! And even if we do have
allies, let us remember that our latent strength
is such that if we prepare it in advance the
chances are strong for our imposing an almost
immediate peace in any conflict into which we
are obliged to enter; whereas if we do not prepare it in advance we are doomed to impotence
in any war unless we have allies who protect
us during the year or two we spend in hurried
and extravagant effort to do what we ought to
have already done.

I am not advocating Prussian militarism. I
am advocating the kind of democratic prepared-

ness which Switzerland has developed to her own great advantage socially and economically, and with the result of keeping war out of her borders. Let us profit by our own experience of the last year. Our training-camps have been universities of applied Americanism. For every young man between the ages of eighteen and twenty to have six months in such a camp, which would include, of course, some field service, would be of incalculable benefit to him, and of like benefit to the nation. It would teach him self-reliance, self-respect, mutuality of respect between himself and others, the power to command and the power to obey; it would teach him habits of cleanliness and order and the power of co-operation, and above all, devotion to the flag, the ideal of country. It would make him a soldier immediately fit for defensive work, and readily to be turned into a soldier fit for offensive work if, as in the present war, offense prove the only method of real defense. Every such man, after his experience in the camp, would tend to be a better citizen and would tend to do his own work for himself and his family better and with more efficient result. His experience would help him in material matters and at the same time would teach him to put certain great spiritual ideals in the foremost place.

Incidentally, we ought to change the draft rules, so far as giving any special privileges to the young fellows between eighteen and twenty in the matter of college training, to fit them to be officers. To say that the nation will pay for all of them to go to college is a deception, and to believe it is a delusion. I do not believe in a selective draft for a favored class. I wish to see fair play for the workman's son who has not had the chance to learn so that he can go to college, but who has the natural ability to command and lead men. Only boys whose parents in the past have had the money to give them a special education can enter college at the present time, and it is unfair to the other boys to give these a special advantage. Let all go into the ranks together and after six months or a year of service let the best men be chosen out to enter the schools which will fit them to be officers. Of course, with the older men and at the beginning, we had to take those already available. But when we come to need the young fellows under twenty-one, let every

man enter the ranks and stand on a fair footing
with every one else, and be given promotion
on his merits.   Hitherto the men who came in
under twenty-one, came in as volunteers, and
they were entitled to try for any position they
could get; but now we have at last done what
we ought to have done in the beginning.   Now
let them all stand alike.

Therefore, I hope that now we shall make the
system of universal military service and military training which we have introduced permanent, although, of course, in modified form.
But I would not stop here.   I would use the
registration of all our men as a basis for further
development for training and service in the
duties of peace.   I would register the young
women just as much as the young men.   I
would give them both certain fundamental
forms of industrial training—training in the
things that are fundamental in the ordinary
work of the ordinary man and woman in their
business occupations and in and around their
home; in the things which it is good for every
man and every woman to know.   I mean certain forms of manual labor and mechanical
labor for men, and certain forms of household

work and work outside of the house for women. The teaching in the schools should be only in English; in this country there is room for but one flag and for but one language. I believe in education. I believe in giving it free to every man and every woman, because I don't think we can have a successful democracy unless it is an educated one. I believe in making it obligatory so far as primary education is concerned, and I believe in making it possible for every man or woman who really desires it to have a higher education, but that this shall be permissive and not obligatory. Moreover, I believe that the education shall be an education not only of the mind but also of the soul and the body. I think we should educate men and women toward and not away from what is to be their life-work—toward the home, toward the farm, toward the shop, and not away from them. I would use the introduction of a system of universal training and service as a means for securing this education.

I mention education only as one of the aims we ought to have in view in connection with universal training of our citizenship for service. There are very many lines of en-

deavor in such an effort of constructive states-
manship; for construction and not destruction
should be the key-note of our policy at this
time. Our educational system should deal
especially with all immigrants; and a peculiarly
important branch of it at the present time
ought to be the training of the disabled and
the crippled returning soldiers, so that they
may become, not objects of charity, but self-
supporting citizens. We should develop the
water-powers under the government, keeping
ownership in the public, and preventing the
pollution of interstate streams. We should
begin at once to take thought for the soldiers
when they return; to develop national employ-
ment agencies for the redistribution of men
after the war. We should enter on a course
of taxation, purchase, and development of
land so as to give to the returned soldier who
is fit for it the chance to do the most vital of
all works, to till the soil on the farm which
he himself owns; and we can treat this as a
stepping-stone to further study of and action
concerning country life and farm production,
so as to promote the growth and prosperity of
the farmers who work hard on their own land.

We must prepare our shipping for times of peace, and prepare to deal with the foreign-markets situation, as part of our programme of wise universal service; and, what is even more important, we must deal on a national scale with factory and industrial conditions; with city and country housing conditions; with child labor; and with old age, health and unemployment insurance for workers.

CHAPTER III

THIS IS THE PEOPLE'S WAR;
PUT IT THROUGH

THIS is the people's war. It is not the President's war. It is not Congress's war. It is America's war. We are in honor bound in conducting it to stand by every official who does well, and against every official who fails to do well. Any other attitude is servile and unworthy of an American freeman.

In the papers ten months ago there appeared a brief statement made by an unnamed young American major to his troops in the trenches in France. He said:

We have reached the top in training. If you need anything come and tell me and I will get it for you if I can. If I do not get it I do not want to hear about it again, for it means that I cannot get it. We will have three meals a day if we can get them. If we have to miss one meal we will not be badly off, and if we miss two or three it will not be much worse. We are expected to work from

midnight of one day to midnight of the next day.
If there is any chance to sleep between, all right.
It will also be all right if there is no chance.   Let
everybody pitch in.   While mud and water must
be fought it may be much worse.   The hopes of
the Nation are fixed on each man.

The ideal of duty thus set before our soldiers, before the Americans who at this time
risk most and suffer most, is substantially the
ideal of duty toward which all of the rest of
us here in America should, in our turn, likewise strive.   We must brace ourselves for effort
and for endurance through a hard and dangerous year.   High of heart and with unfaltering
soul, we must do our part in the grim work of
toiling and fighting to bring a little nearer the
day when there shall be orderly liberty throughout the world, and when justice and mercy and
brotherly love shall obtain between man and
man and among all the nations of mankind.
We must show our faith by our works.   We
must prove our truth by our endeavor.   We
must scorn the baseness which uses high-
sounding speech to cloak ignoble action, and
which seeks to betray suffering right with the
Judas kiss of a treacherous peace.

Henceforth we at home will suffer some dis-
comfort, a little unimportant privation and
much wearing anxiety. What of it? What
we at home endure will be as nothing compared to that which is faced by the sons and
brothers, by the husbands and fathers at the
front; and what the fighting men of to-day
face and bear will be no harder than what was
faced and borne by Washington's troops at
Valley Forge and Trenton, and by the soldiers of Grant and Lee when they wrestled in
the Wilderness. We inherit as free men this
fair and mighty land only because our fathers
and forefathers had iron in their blood. We
can leave our heritage undiminished to those
who come after us only if we in our turn show
a resolute and rugged manliness in the dark
days of trial that have come upon us.

Let us all, individually and collectively, do
our whole duty with brave hearts. Let us pay
our taxes, subscribe to the government loans,
work at our several tasks with all our strength,
support all the agencies which take care of
our troops and accept the stinting in fuel or
food as part of the price we pay. Let our
prime care be the welfare and warlike efficiency

of the men at the front and in the training-camps. Let us hold to sharp account every public servant who, in any way, comes short of his duty in this respect. But let us also insist that the soldiers at the front and in the camps treat every shortcoming merely as an obstacle to be overcome or remedied or offset by their own energy and courage and resourcefulness. The one absolute essential for our people is to insist that this war be seen through at no matter what cost, until it is crowned with the peace of overwhelming victory for the right.

There are foolish persons who still say we ought to make peace now, a negotiated peace, and then be good friends with Germany. These persons with all the lessons of the last four years fresh in their minds still cling pathetically to the belief that if only we will show that we are harmless Germany will begin to love us.

As a matter of fact, the German hatred of America grew to be a positive obsession during the two and a half years of our ignoble and cold-blooded neutrality, when we submitted feebly to all the German wrong-doing. Let

the foolish persons who doubt this read the
books written by Mr. Gerard, our ambassador
at Berlin, and the book written by Mr. Gibson,
secretary of our legation at Brussels. Still
better let them read the articles by Mr. Curtis
Roth, until recently vice-consul at Plauen,
Saxony.

These writings show the extent of the hatred
with which Germany regards America, a hatred
which blossomed into full growth before we
went to war, and which was immensely aggravated because of the contempt inspired by our
tame submission to outrage for over two years.
Mr. Roth's testimony is peculiarly interesting.
He shows that Berlin actively stimulated the
campaign of hatred and revenge against America, that the German people accepted the view
that Americans were cowardly, avaricious, and
effeminate, that they singled out for hatred
the German-Americans beyond all other American citizens, and that in Germany it was con-
stantly announced that sooner or later there
would be a day of reckoning when America
would have to pay a huge indemnity or suffer
the fate of Belgium. Mr. Roth shows that
the German people think exactly as their lead-

ers think and that they now hate and despise us Americans as they hate no others of their foes, not even the English. Says Mr. Roth: "They resolved to make our country drink to the depths out of the bitter cup of humiliation." Nothing do they find more despicable than our talk about peace, which they attributed to cowardice and flabbiness. They look on the American pacifist as a weakling and as a God-given tool in the hands of German interests.

Ambassador Gerard reported the German state of mind again and again; in October, 1915, he specifically reported the Kaiser's threat to stand no nonsense from America, and exact full payment from her; but President Wilson kept the American people ignorant of the facts, and unprepared to defend their rights. In practice President Wilson holds to secret diplomacy, to secretive and furtive diplomacy, with a tenacity as marked as the fluency with which in theory he champions its abolition.

All Americans who were both thoroughly patriotic and well-informed lifted their heads with pride when at last this nation did what it would have been infinitely better to have done two years previously—when at last it went to

war. There were well-meaning men who had
been misled as to our duty, or who lacked
vision, and who in consequence were even at
that time against our going into the war. But
the great majority of these men are now as
patriotic as any one else; and all patriotic and
far-sighted Americans must now sternly insist
that the war be carried through to a completely
victorious conclusion, at no matter what cost of
blood and treasure, and no matter how long
the time. All those who now ask for an inde-
cisive peace, all who now assail our allies or
directly or indirectly apologize for or give aid
and comfort to Germany, all who do not insist
upon the utmost speed and thorough efficiency
in the conduct of the war, are false to America
and false to all the liberty-loving nations of
mankind.

Germany respects only force. She rightly
considers the sentimentality (I am not talking
of sentiment) which clamors for peace without
punishing her brutality and perfidy, as a mere
cloak for cowardice and lazy weakness. Every
man in this country who now advocates Germany's cause, whether directly or indirectly,
or who demands a negotiated, inconclusive

peace without victory, is not only treacherously false to this country, but is earning Germany's utter derision for himself and for our country in so far as it is influenced by him.   Mr. Roth sums up by saying that "the average German hates this country to-day with a hatred far more venomous, far more implacable, far more unreasoning than the hatred he has visited upon any other people."   Remember that this hatred has come upon us because for two years and a half we were neutral, because by failing to stand up for our own rights we lost the respect of Germany, because by our failing to prepare we incurred her utter contempt, because she despised and despises us for our weakness in dealing with the pro-Germans here at home.   There is but one way to gain the respect of the Prussianized, militarist, and autocratic Germany of the Hohenzollerns, and that is by beating her to her knees.   And in order to beat her as thoroughly and speedily as possible we should treat with drastic severity the Hun within our own gates.

CHAPTER IV

THE SQUARE DEAL IN AMERICANISM

THERE are two demands upon the spirit of Americanism, of nationalism. Each must be met. Each is essential. Each is vital, if we are to be a great and proud nation.

The first is that we shall tolerate no kind of divided allegiance in this country. There is no room for the hyphen in our citizenship. There is no place for a 50–50 Americanism in the United States. He who is not with us, absolutely and without reserve of any kind, is against us, and should be treated as an alien enemy, to be interned or sent out of the country. We have room in this country for but one flag, the Stars and Stripes, and we should tolerate no allegiance to any other flag, whether a foreign flag or the red flag or black flag. We have room for but one loyalty, loyalty to the United States. We have room for but one language, the language of Washington and

Lincoln, the language of the Declaration of Independence and the Gettysburg speech; the English language. English should be the only language used or taught in the primary schools, public or private; in higher schools of learning other modern languages should be taught, on an equality with one another; but the language of use and instruction should be English. We should require by law that within a reasonable length of time, a time long enough to prevent needless hardship, every newspaper should be published in English. The language of the church and the Sunday-school should be English. The government should provide night schools free for every immigrant who comes here, require him to attend them, and return him to his own country unless at the end of five years he has learned to speak and read English. This war has shown us in vivid and startling fashion the danger of allowing our people to separate along lines of racial origin and linguistic cleavage. We shall be guilty of criminal folly if we fail to insist on the complete and thoroughgoing unification of our people.

The German-American Alliance and all similar bodies, the Sinn Feiners, the East Side Russian revolutionary organizations, the Germanized Socialists, and most of the leaders of Mr. Townley's Non-Partisan League and the I. W. W. are anti-American to the core. In *Everybody's Magazine* for December last will be found extracts from German-American papers, and from Sinn Fein and Yiddish pro-German papers which are as profoundly anti-American as if they were published in Berlin. It is true that parallel with them are given extracts just as mischievous from certain papers printed in English, like the Hearst papers. Morally the latter are even more to blame than the former; but in their case the evil teaching is at any rate in a language which permits us to know about it, and to act about it if we choose; whereas the foreign-language papers work behind a veil which shuts them out from the sight of the average citizen.

There is no permanent use in half-measures. It is silly to be lackadaisical over men of German origin having to fight the Germans of Prussianized Germany. Washington and most of his associates were of English origin; nevertheless they fought the British King. If they had not done so we would not now be a nation. If the Americans of German blood do not now fight against Germany and feel against Germany as strongly as the rest of us they are not fit to be Americans at all. The deeds committed by King George and his servants which led up to the Revolution were trivial compared to the hideous iniquities perpetrated upon us by the servants, tools, and agents of the Hohenzollerns during the last four years. If peace should come to-morrow, nevertheless our bitter experience should teach us for a generation to watch keenly for German propaganda in this country, to treat with contemptuous scorn the Hearsts, Vierecks, and the like, and to crush under our heel every movement that smacks in the smallest degree of playing the German game.

This is one of the demands to be made in the name of the spirit of American nationalism. The other is equally important. We must treat every good American of German or of any other origin, without regard to his creed, as on a full and exact equality with every other good American, and set our faces like flint against the creatures who seek to discriminate against such an American, or to hold against him the birthplace of himself or his parents. The friends of whom I am proudest and in whom I most believe include men like Loeb and Herman Hagedorn and Hans Zinser and Dolge, and the late George Meyer and August Vogel, and innumerable others, who are themselves in the army, or whose sons are in the army, and whose patriotism entitles them to fill any position from the presidency down. To discriminate in any way, because they are in whole or in part of German blood, against such men as these, who are typical Americans of the very best kind this country yields, is a base infamy from the personal standpoint, and from the public standpoint is utterly un-American and profoundly un-patriotic. Among the Americans who have won most honor at the front are very many of German blood. The battalions, companies, squadrons, and batteries which my sons command, and have commanded, are full of such men. There is no better officer or more typical American in the entire American navy than my former White House aide, Osterhaus. I read how Lieutenant Edward Rickenbacher, the crack flier of our air service, attacked single-handed and destroyed two German airplanes, and then on his way back across our lines saw a fellow American flier, Lieutenant James A. Meissner, assailed by a German airplane while he was attacking another; and Rickenbacher brought down the latter, and the two Americans returned in triumph. From their names I gather that the two men are at least in part of German blood (as I am myself). They have made all good Americans their debtors!

The other day I spoke at Springfield, Ohio, for speeding up the war until Germany was beaten to her knees. I was introduced by the President of Wittenberg College, a Lutheran college founded by Germans, but now straight-out American, just as much as Harvard, Yale, or Princeton, with two hundred of her sons in our army or navy. The invocation was by a Catholic monsignor, a chaplain-major in the United States army, born in Germany; the benediction was by a Lutheran minister of German parentage. But we were all four of us Americans and nothing else, and we all preached the same straight-out doctrine of simon-pure Americanism—and in the same language, English. At Martinsville, Ind., I was introduced by Mayor Schmidt, whose two sons were in the army; one·was wounded and was in the same hospital with one of my sons. At Milwaukee, I was introduced by August Vogel; three of his sons were in the army, and the fourth was only waiting until he was eighteen. In one hospital on the cot next to another of my sons was another young officer, wounded also. He had shown exceptional gallantry; and when a Red Cross worker asked him his name he answered: "Say! Don't faint! My name is Von Holzendorf. Wouldn't the Huns feel gay if they knew they had almost got a man of that name?" The troops commanded by my sons have included at least as many men whose parents were born in foreign countries—England and Ireland, Germany, France, Belgium, Italy, and the Scandinavian and Slavonic lands—as men whose parents were of old native American stock; some were Protestants, some Catholics, some Jews; and all did equally well, and all were Americans and nothing but Americans.

I read in the press how the New York Liederkranz has established English as the official language of the club, and passed a resolution providing for the expulsion of any member of the club who is guilty directly or indirectly of an act or word hostile to the United States or its allies. As its president said, the club is "100 per cent American"; and between one and two hundred of its members or their sons and nephews now wear the uniform of the United States army or navy.

Indeed the club has thought of changing its name. This I hope will not be done. "German" should be left out of the name; but Liederkranz is just as good a name for a club as Knickerbocker, just as good a name as is William and Mary for a college; and I think it a mistake to lose the sense of historic continuity by abandoning any such name, which has grown to possess many American associations. Moreover, the Liederkranz type of club is one which, when thoroughly Americanized, and when Americans of all national origins are admitted freely into it, and when developed along our own lines, makes a distinctly individual and most valuable contribution to American social life.

So it is with the best type of "German-

American" newspaper. Many of these papers have a fine and honorable record. At this moment such a paper as the *New-Yorker Herold* is doing capital work; and it was founded by a "forty-eighter" who stanchly upheld Lincoln and the cause of the Union and of Liberty. There is just one way by which to preserve *in its usefulness* such a paper, and that is to have it gradually change from German into English. If it continues German it will either die or cease to be useful to the country. For example, the *Brooklyner Freie Presse* has just suspended publication, because, in spite of its patriotism, its patriotic readers grew to wish to read papers printed in the tongue of their fellow countrymen. It was founded by a German, a Union soldier; four of his grandsons are now in the military service of the United States. The big press associations of the country should step in and patriotically offer their services for English editions of such papers if they will change from German to English. Every paper in a foreign language should be required to be published in English after a reasonable time; but many such papers are entirely loyal and have been

very useful; and we should make every effort
to enable them to continue as American newspapers, proud of their past, but changed as
the changing times require, and henceforth
printed in the language of the American people.

When I was Governor of New York I was a
member of the same Dutch Reformed church
to which two and a half centuries earlier
Governor Peter Stuyvesant had belonged;
and we sat at communion at a long table in the
aisle just as he and his associates had done.
It was pleasant, indeed wise, to keep alive
the tradition, the sense of historic continuity.
But we used English, not Dutch, as our language; our minister had a Scotch name; one-
half the congregation had English or other
non-Dutch names. We were not exiled or
transplanted Hollanders. We were Americans
and nothing but Americans; we were at
home in America, and only in America.

Many politicians and many newspapers,
actuated by varying motives, have upheld the
theory of separate nationalities in America—
a theory absolutely fatal to true Americanism. Recently the New York *World* was
quoted as demanding the stopping of "the

crusade against German language newspapers" on the ground that "we need the true Germany in America to fight the false Germany in Europe." There could be no demand more mischievously unpatriotic and anti-American. It is precisely the demand which a far-seeing Ambassador Bernstorff would most warmly encourage. We do not need a "Germany in America," whether true or false, any more than we need an "England in America," or an "Ireland in America," or any other nation-of-somewhere-else in America. To encourage "the true Germany in America" is to encourage a separate nationality within our borders, which may at any time define "truth" and "falseness" in terms not of America but of Germany. No good citizen or true American will accept the *World's* position in this matter. We must resolutely refuse to permit our great nation, our great America, to be split into a score of little replicas of European nationalities, and to become a Balkan Peninsula on a larger scale. We are a nation, and not a hodge-podge of foreign nationalities. We are a people, and not a polyglot boarding-house. We must insist on a unified nationality, with one flag, one language, one set of national ideals. We must shun as we would shun the plague all efforts to make us separate in groups of separate nationalities. We must all of us be Americans, and nothing but Americans; and all good Americans must stand on an equality of consideration and respect, without regard to their creed or to the land from which their forebears came.

Elsie Singmaster, whose writings, perhaps especially those dealing with the battle of Gettysburg, are sermons teaching what is best and simplest and loftiest in the American spirit, has written me a letter setting forth what I have to say better than I can do it myself.

GETTYSBURG, PA., June 3, 1918.

MY DEAR COLONEL ROOSEVELT:

I have been reading with pleasure an account of your timely address to the Germans of Milwaukee, and it occurred to me that you might be interested in the earliest piece of similar advice, which I enclose herewith. It is a great pity that there were so few early and later German Americans of Pastorius's mind.

Since 1914 I have taken pains to observe the attitude of the Pennsylvania Germans, and I believe that the majority are as heartily in favor of this war as any other good Americans. A "foreign German" in a Pennsylvania German village has for generations been as much of an alien as an Italian or a Spaniard and has had less in common with the inhabitants.

Last month I spoke each evening in some little church or school house of our county for our local Red Cross organization, and I am beginning to feel that we are a nation aroused. To drive miles on a mountain road which seems to be really a creek bed, to speak to a handful of people, to be listened to with attention which not even the calling of the whip-poor-wills outside or the wailing of the babies within can affect in the least, and then to watch an old man, poor in worldly goods, but rich in patriotism, rise to give the first five or ten dollars of a generous donation because he "went out in '61 and stayed till the end and wants to help the boys now"—there is an experience to be remembered always.

Very sincerely yours,
ELSIE SINGMASTER LEWARS.

The letter of Pastorius to his children, written in 1695, runs in part as follows: the advice was sound then (at the time when certain of my own forebears who were German or "high Dutch" were helping found Germantown), and it is even sounder now, when the opportunity is to become not English colonists but American citizens.

Dear Children: John, Samuel and Henry Pastorius: Though you are (*Germano sanguine nati*) of high Dutch parents, yet remember that your father was Naturalized, and ye born in an English colony, Consequently each of you *Anglus Natus* an Englishmen by Birth. Therefore it would be a shame for you if you should be ignorant of the English tongue, the tongue of your Countrymen; but that you may learn the better I have left a Book for you both, and commend the same to your reiterated perusal. If you should not get much of the Latin, nevertheless read ye the English part oftentimes OVER AND OVER AND OVER. For the drippings of the house-eaves in time make a hole in a hard stone.

Treat all Americans as on the same footing; and let no man live permanently in this country unless he is an American and nothing but an American.

We are the fellow countrymen of Washington and Lincoln, of Lighthorse Harry Lee and his great son, of Grant and Sherman and Farragut, of Marion and Paul Revere and Schuyler, of Washington's General Sullivan and

Lincoln's General Sheridan. These men were of diverse ancestry; their forefathers came from England or Ireland or Scotland or Holland or France or Spain. But they were Americans, and nothing else; and if we are really to be loyal to their spirit, we, in our day, must be Americans, and nothing else. And, above all, we must be Americans, and only Americans, in the face of any and every foreign foe.

We are also, and just as much, the fellow countrymen of Muhlenberg and Custer. There is no more typically American figure in the Revolutionary War than that of Muhlenberg, the American of pure German blood, the pastor of a Lutheran church at the outbreak of the Revolution. On the Sunday after the call for arms came he mounted his pulpit; he admonished his flock that there was a time for prayer and a time for battle, and that the time for battle had come. Casting aside his frock, he appeared in the uniform of a colonel of the Continental Army; and on many a stricken field he proved his valor and devotion. Custer, a man of German descent, was one of the most gallant and heroic figures of the Civil War and the Indian Wars; his name and career made up one of the finest traditions of our army. In the Civil War there fought many, many men of German birth; Sigel, Osterhaus, Hentzleman; innumerable others. They proved their Americanism by their deeds. Their grandsons are in our armies and navy to-day. Their undivided loyalty is given to one flag, to our flag. They are incapable of a loyalty different from that of their fellow Americans of different blood. These fellow Americans of theirs who happen to be of different blood must in their turn see to it that any one who discriminates against these men because they are of German blood is himself branded as a traitor.

I speak as an American who has German blood in his veins. I speak on behalf of all loyal Americans who are, in whole or in part, of German blood. Our devotion knows no other country but this. With all our hearts we are against Germany to-day exactly as the loyal Americans of English descent who followed Washington were against England in their day. We feel it incumbent on us to be, if anything, a little more ready to follow the call of America against Germany precisely because of our blood. Our hearts burn with wrath over the horrible brutality, cruelty, and treachery of the Germany of the Hohenzollerns. We abhor, and would punish with relentless sternness, the American traitors of German blood who in this crisis are false to America, or hostile to the Allies of America, or who in any way or shape serve Germany. And therefore we feel the keenest indignation against all men who in any way seek to discriminate against us because of the land from which our forefathers came. We do not beg as a favor, we challenge as a right, full equality of respect and of treatment for all our fellow Americans.

I have just received a letter from one of the very best Americans I know, a Congregational clergyman, Frazer Metzger, a man whose father and mother both were born in Germany. He was an exceptionally high-minded and useful citizen in time of peace. Since this war began his soul has flamed with anger against the ruthless wickedness of Germany; and he has led with fiery ardor in every patriotic movement to strengthen America's hands and to exalt her soul so that she may accept no peace without overwhelming victory. Yet mean-souled creatures have assailed this man because he is of German blood. He writes me:

This distrust is putting fear into the hearts of some of us, which fear is not personal but national. I understand that Washington looks upon Goethals as pro-German, and I can't believe it. Take my own case. Since the outbreak of the war, I have devoted practically all my time and spent all my little savings for America and against the indescribable menace of German dominance. Yet I find myself laid open to the suspicion of being pro-German, charged with hiding my German proclivities behind a blatant and insincere loyalty, merely because I am of German descent.

The people who thus assail a high-minded American because he is of German blood are as base as if they slandered the memories of Nathan Hale and his New England comrades of the Revolution because they were of English blood. The finest Americans in our land to-day are the Americans of German blood whose whole-hearted loyalty is given to this Republic as against all her foes. One of the ablest and most gallant men in our army, born in Germany, recently wrote me: "Your country is my country, and my country is your country, and there is no other country for either of us." There spoke the true American! How can we sufficiently express our scorn of those who would in any way discriminate against such Americans?

The persons who attempt such discrimination are themselves utterly unpatriotic. By their actions they inflict a cruel wrong on their fellow countrymen. Moreover, they do their best to drive these same fellow countrymen away from their loyalty. There are plenty of men of German blood who are disloyal; and there are plenty of men of Irish and Jewish *and native-American* blood who are disloyal— indeed, the most influential leaders of disloyalty in this country have been of old native stock. Punish every disloyal man; but punish him because he is disloyal, not because of his blood. The government ought at once to establish martial law wherever there are outrages against person or property by German spies or by pro-German American sympathizers, or by Irishmen whose hatred of England makes them disloyal to America, or by I. W. W. people, or by any other enemies of our country. The government ought to visit all such offenders with the full severity of military law. The time for shilly-shallying is long past. Any newspaper, whether published in German or in English, which directly or indirectly supports traitorous action should be promptly suppressed. But the great mass of Americans who are wholly or partly of German blood are exactly as loyal as Americans of any other blood; and it is a foul wrong not to treat all exactly alike.

I am well aware that the trouble is mainly due to the action of the openly or covertly disloyal German-Americans and of the openly or covertly disloyal German-American press, and of the Irish-Americans who are the paid or unpaid agents of Germany, and of the native American politicians and editors who have pandered to the disloyal foreign vote. Among all these paid or unpaid agents of Germany, the disloyal men of German origin have been the most evil enemies of the entirely loyal mass of American citizens of German origin; and this should be recognized by all loyal citizens.

The disloyal man, whether his disloyalty

is open or disguised, is our worst foe; but close behind him comes the man who, whether from wickedness or foolishness, assails his loyal fellow citizens because of the blood that flows in their veins.

Indeed, this war against the brutal militaristic and capitalistic tyranny of Germany is, in a sense, peculiarly the war of all true Americans of German blood, exactly as the war of the Revolution was, in a sense, peculiarly the war of all true Americans of English blood. It should mark the rebirth of our nation; of a nation dedicated to orderly freedom and to the cause of justice for all men. We are a new people; we differ from all other peoples; we are neither English nor Irish, neither German nor French; we are Americans, and only Americans. We are bound to treat all other nations on their conduct, and only on their conduct, in each crisis as it arises.

Above all, we are bound to treat all our fellow Americans with reference solely to their whole-hearted loyalty to American ideals as embodied in the great Americans whose names I have used above. True Americans who are in whole or in part of Germany blood claim nothing except the right to serve America and to be judged according to their service.

Just what and who the American fighting man—and therefore the best American—is when at his best, may be seen in the following poem by Mr. James W. Foley. Many years ago, in the cow country, on the Little Missouri, Mr. Foley's father was a valued friend and neighbor of mine; and the poet himself was the "Foley's boy" of the Ann Arbor Professor incident, recorded on page 426 of my "Wilderness Hunter." The poem runs as follows:

YANKS

O'Leary, from Chicago, and a first-class fightin'
    man,
For his father was from Kerry, where the gentle
    art began:
Sergeant Dennis P. O'Leary, from somewhere on
    Archie Road,
Dodgin' shells and smellin' powder while the battle
    ebbed and flowed.

And the captain says: "O'Leary, from your fight-
    in' company
Pick a dozen fightin' Yankees and come skirmishin'
    with me;

Pick a dozen fightin' devils, and I know it's you
who can."
And O'Leary, he saluted like a first-class fightin'
man.

O'Leary's eye was piercin' and O'Leary's voice
was clear:
"Dimitri Georgoupoulos!" And Dimitri answered
"Here!"
Then "Vladimir Slaminsky! Step three paces
to the front,
For we're wantin' you to join us in a little Heinie
hunt!"

"Garibaldi Ravioli!" Garibaldi was to share;
And "Ole Axel Kettleson!" and "Thomas Scalp-
the-Bear!"
Who was Choctaw by inheritance, bred in the blood
and bones,
But set down in army records by the name of
Thomas Jones.

"Van Winkle Schuyler Stuyvesant!" Van Winkle
was a bud
From the ancient tree of Stuyvesant and had it in
his blood;
"Don Miguel de Colombo!" Don Miguel's next
kin
Were across the Rio Grande when Don Miguel
went in.

"Ulysses Grant O'Sheridan!" Ulysses' sire, you
   see,
Had been at Appomattox near the famous apple-
   tree;
And "Patrick Michael Casey!" Patrick Michael,
   you can tell,
Was a fightin' man by nature with three fightin'
   names as well.

"Joe Wheeler Lee!" And Joseph had a pair of
   fightin' eyes;
And his granddad was a Johnny, as perhaps you
   might surmise;
Then "Robert Bruce MacPherson!" And the
   Yankee squad was done
With "Isaac Abie Cohen!" once a lightweight
   champion.

Then O'Leary paced 'em forward and, says he:
   "You Yanks, fall in!"
And he marched 'em to the captain. "Let the
   skirmishin' begin.
Says he, "The Yanks are comin', and you beat
   'em if you can!"
And saluted like a soldier and first-class fightin'
   man!

By rights this skirmish squad should have
included a couple of men of German parentage,
and two or three others whose ancestors came

over in the *Mayflower;* and then it would have been an accurate cross-section of the American people. This war has been the real crucible, the functioning crucible for our nation; and now no matter what our ancestry, all of us who are Americans at all are Americans and nothing else.

CHAPTER V

SOUND NATIONALISM AND SOUND INTERNATIONALISM

THE tremendous thrust of the Allies during the last three months, in which the hard-fighting soldiers of the American army have borne so distinguished and honorable a part, has meant grave military disaster to Germany. Therefore it has resulted in a renewal of the German peace offensive. No man can prophesy in these matters; but the Germans may yet continue the war for a long time; and therefore we should prepare to have in France an army of four million fighting men (not including non-combatants) for the battle front next spring. But the Germans seem likely to try to make peace instead of continuing the war and are apparently seeking to cover their retention of some of their ill-gotten substantial gains by nominal and theoretical support of some glittering proposal about a league of nations to end all war. They thereby hope to keep part of their booty by appealing to what is vaguely called internationalism, and getting the support not only of sentimentalists who do not like to look unpleasant facts in the face, but also of the good people who are appalled and puzzled and panic-stricken by the horror Germany has brought on the world, and who, instead of bracing themselves to put down this horror by their own hardened strength and iron will, clutch at any quack remedy which false prophets hold out as offering a substitute for such action.

Therefore it is well at this time for sober and resolute men and women to apply that excellent variety of wisdom colloquially known as "horse-sense" to the problems of nationalism and internationalism. These problems will not be solved by rhetoric. Least of all will they be solved by competitive rhetoric. Masters of phrasemaking may win immense, although evanescent, applause by outvying one another in words that glitter, but these glittering words will not have one shred of lasting effect on the outcome except in so far as they may have a very mischievous effect if they persuade good, ignorant people to aban-

don the possible real good in the fantastic effort
to achieve an impossible unreal perfection. Let
honest men and women remember that this kind
of phrasemongering does not represent idealism.
The only idealism worth considering in the
workaday business of this world is applied
idealism. This is merely another way of saying that permanent good to humanity is most
apt to come from actually trying to reduce
ideals to practice, and this means that the
ideals must be substantially or at least measur-
ably realizable.

The professed internationalist usually sneers
at nationalism, at patriotism, and at what we
call Americanism. He bids us forswear our
love of country in the name of love of the
world at large. We nationalists answer that
he has begun at the wrong end; we say that,
as the world now is, it is only the man who
ardently loves his country first who in actual
practice can help any other country at all.
The internationalist bids us to promise to
abandon the idea of keeping America permanently ready to defend her rights by her
strength and to trust, instead, to scraps of
paper, to written agreements by which all

nations form a league, and agree to disarm, and agree each to treat all other nations, big or little, on an exact equality. We nationalists answer that we are ready to join any league to enforce peace or similar organization which offers a likelihood of in some measure lessening the number and the area of future wars, but only on condition that in the first place we do not promise what will not or ought not to be performed, or be guilty of proclaiming a sham, and that in the second place we do not surrender our right and duty to prepare our own strength for our own defense instead of trusting to the above-mentioned scraps of paper. In justification we point to certain very obvious facts which ought to be patent to every man of common sense.

Any such league of nations must, of course, include the nine nations which have the greatest military strength, or it will be utterly impotent. These nine nations include Germany, Austria, Turkey, and Russia. The first three have abundantly shown during the last four years that no written or other promise of the most binding kind has even the slightest effect upon their actions. The fourth, Russia, under the lead and dominion of the Bolsheviki, has just been guilty of the grossest possible betrayal of her Allies and of the small kindred Slavonic peoples and of world democracy. This betrayal was in the interest of a military and despotic autocracy and included the direct violation of Russia's plighted faith. Under such conditions it is unnecessary to say that at present Russia's signature to a league to enforce peace will not be worth the paper on which it is written. Therefore the creation of any such league for the future will simply mean a pledge by the present Allies to make their alliance perpetual, and all to go to war again whenever one of them is attacked. This may become necessary, but it certainly does not imply future disarmament. And if the administration really means loyal adherence to a league of nations, or a league to enforce peace in the future, it must at once confess and atone for its shameful betrayal of the existing league of Allies by its failure to declare war on Turkey and Bulgaria.

Nor is this all. The United States must come into court with clean hands. She must not pledge herself without reservation to the

right of "self-determination" for each people
while she has behaved toward Haiti and San
Domingo as she is now behaving. It is not
possible for me to say whether our action in
these two cases has been right or wrong, because the administration, with its usual horror
of publicity, whether pitiless or otherwise,
and its inveterate predilection for secret and
furtive diplomacy, has kept most of the facts
hidden. I believe that there was no possible
excuse for such secret diplomacy in these cases
and that the same course should have been
followed as was followed in the case of the
Panama Revolution, where every fact was immediately laid without reservation before Congress (and where, incidentally, what this country did was merely to give Panama the "right
of self-determination" of which we have robbed
Haiti and San Domingo). But even if I am
wrong in my belief in the general principle
of open diplomacy, and even if the administration is right in its consistent policy of secret
diplomacy as regards the mass of questions
which I think ought to be made public, the
fact remains that we have with armed force
invaded, made war upon, and conquered the

two small republics, have upset their governments, have denied them the right of self-determination, and have made democracy within their limits not merely unsafe but non-existent. As we have no published facts to go on, I cannot say whether their misconduct did or did not warrant such drastic action on our part. But on the assumption that the administration acted properly, we are committed to the principle that some nations are not fit for self-determination, that democracy within their limits is a sham, and that their offenses against justice and right are such as to render interference by their more powerful and more civilized neighbors imperative. I do not doubt that this principle is true in some cases, whether or not it ought to be applied in these two particular cases. In any event our continuing action in San Domingo and Haiti makes it hypocritical for us to lay down any universal rules about self-determination for all nations. Moreover, our destruction of democracy in these two little republics, whether justifiable or not, makes it hypocritical of the administration to profess that it purposes to "make democracy safe" throughout the world.

Our action also shows how utterly futile it would be to try to treat a league to enforce peace as a substitute for training our own strength for our own defense. Let China be the witness of the truth of this statement. China has actually realized the ideal of the pacifists who insist that unpreparedness for war secures peace. The ideal of the internationalists is that patriotism and the sense of nationalism are detrimental to humanity, and the ideal of the socialists is that the capitalist régime is the only cause of popular misery. China is helpless to attack others or defend herself, her people have little sense of national unity and pride, and there are in China huge districts where there are no capitalists, and where the misery of the people is greater than in any country of the Occident. China's helplessness, instead of helping toward world peace, has been a positive encouragement to war and violence among her neighbors. Her future depends primarily not on herself but on what her neighbors choose to do. In spite of her size and her enormous population and resources she is helpless to do good to others because she is powerless to prevent others from doing evil to her. Her agreement to a league of nations or to a league to enforce peace would be worthless because she is unable to put strength back of justice either for herself or for any one else. The pacifists and internationalists, if they had their way, would turn the United States into the China of the Occident.

Let us put our trust neither in rhetoric nor hypocrisy, whether conscious or unconscious. Let us be honest with ourselves. Let us look the truth in the face. Let us remember what Germany, Austria, and Turkey have actually done. Let us remember what Russia has suffered from Germany and the worse than folly with which she has behaved to every one else. Let us remember what has happened to China, and what we have made happen to Haiti and San Domingo. Then let us trust for our salvation to a sound and intense American nationalism.

The horse-sense of the matter is that all agreements to further the cause of sound internationalism must be based on recognition of the fact that, as the world is actually constituted, our present prime need is this sound and intense American nationalism. The first essential of this sound nationalism is that the nation shall trust to its own fully prepared strength for its own defense. So far as possible, its strength must also be used to secure justice for others and must never be used to wrong others. But unless we possess and prepare the strength, we can neither help ourselves nor others. Let us by all means go into any wise league or covenant among nations to abolish neutrality (for of course a league to enforce peace is merely another name for a league to abolish neutrality in every possible war). But let us first understand what we are promising, and count the cost and determine to keep our promises. Above all, let us treat any such agreement or covenant as a mere addition or supplement to and never as a substitute for the preparation in advance of our own armed power. Next time that we behave with the ignoble folly we have shown during the last four years we may not find allies to do what France and England and Italy have done for us. They have protected us with their navies and armies, their blood and their treasure, while we first refused to do anything and then slowly and reluctantly began to harden and make ready our giant but soft and lazy strength.

No paper scheme designed to secure peace without effort and safety without service and sacrifice will either make this country safe or enable it to do its international duty toward others.

An American citizen, personally unknown to me, writes me that his three sons entered the army at the outbreak of the war and that one of them, an aviator, was killed in battle at the front just two weeks before my own son was killed as he fought in the air. In his letter my correspondent adds:

Would that my country might learn and never forget that not only the winning of peace now, but the maintenance of peace at all times depends not fundamentally on treaties or leagues of nations, but on the readiness of citizens to fly to the aid of the wronged and to give their lives if need be that justice may be secured.

There speaks the true American spirit which holds fast alike to fearlessness and to wisdom, to gentleness and to iron resolution. There speaks the spirit of that fervent nationalism which would forbid America either to inflict or to endure wrong.

The cult of absolute internationalism *as a substitute for nationalism* is the cult of a doctrine of fatal sterility. It had much vogue up to the beginning of this war among the professional "intellectuals," especially among bright, clever young college men of superficial cultivation. It was of real damage to these, and therefore it, to a certain extent, damaged the country; for it inevitably emasculates its sincere votaries, and therefore deprives their country of whatever aid they could otherwise give in the effort to build a vigorous civilization, based, as every civilization worth calling such must be, on a spirit of intense nationalism.

The damage done, because of the way such sham internationalism destroys the creative fibre of the intellectuals, is chiefly of negative character. It deprives the nation of a growth-force which ought to be a valuable asset. But it works in positively mischievous fashion among the powerful sinister men who are not sincere devotees of the cult, but who use it as a cloak behind which they war on all civilization, or else deliberately adopt a pretense of belief in it in order to weaken other nations and make them an easier prey. The Russian Bolshevists embody the first of these attitudes. The German Socialists embody the second. In the United States the I. W. W. and all anarchists of that stamp take essentially the position of the Russian Bolshevists; while the American Socialist party, which is a mere annex of Germany, follows the lead of the German Socialists.

There are a few high-minded Socialists in America who have refused to bow the knee to Baal, who denounce the German Socialists, and uphold the great war for human freedom against Germany. But they are very, very few. They have been contemptuously thrust aside by the Socialist party organization. Under the actual conditions their continued assertion of their belief in "internationalism" has a merely pathetic significance.

The great majority of the Socialist, Bolshevist, and other big organizations which before the war had most loudly declared their allegiance to "internationalism," have during the last four years sinned against international fair

dealing and justice more heavily than any
other groups of men in the world, save only
the Prussianized people of Germany and the
rulers of Turkey. If sound internationalism
means anything it means insisting upon justice
between nations and condemning wrong done
by one nation to another. But the German
Socialists, who had loudly preached "internationalism," have eagerly supported the German autocracy in its course of international
robbery and murder, and have cynically announced that they only preached pacifism to
other nations in order to make them the easier
victims of German militarism; the Socialist
David announcing in the Reichstag: "Germany must squeeze her enemies with a pair of
pinchers, the military pincher and the pacifist
pincher. The German armies must continue to
fight vigorously while the German Socialists
encourage and stimulate pacifism among Germany's enemies." This was the real result of
professional internationalism in Germany—a
resolute attempt to convert all free nations into
the vassals of Germany. Meanwhile, in America, in France, in England, and in Italy, either
the majority or else a large minority of the

avowed "international" Socialists, were putting a premium on Germany's crimes against international justice by refusing to condemn them, by clamoring against war with Germany, and by clamoring for a peace which would leave Germany unpunished. Then in Russia the extreme professional internationalists, the Bolshevists, got control. They instantly betrayed the cause of international right and justice, behaving with a venal contempt of decency which makes the Holy Alliance of the sovereigns who overthrew Napoleon seem respectable by comparison. They greedily sold themselves and their country for German gold, they aided the German propaganda, they deserted their allies, the free nations, they tore Russia in pieces, they butchered their fellow countrymen by tens of thousands. They have done all in their power to fasten the German yoke on the whole world, and they have done it in the name of "internationalism"!

This is what happened in actual practice as soon as the "international" parties began to apply the "internationalism" they had so vehemently preached. The visionaries and enthusiasts among the internationalist leaders have been merely the tools of two sets of evil beings; the brutish creatures who wished to destroy all government, and especially all good government, because they are themselves fit only for the slime of the pit and hate the light and all who dwell in the light; and the astute sordid creatures who serve their own self-interest by serving Germany, whether for downright pay or for other considerations, and who find that the easiest way to render such service is to weaken their own countries, and to debase civilization, by breaking down the spirit of patriotism and nationalism under pretense of supporting internationalism.

When these are the fruits of applied internationalism, how is it possible for any high-minded man, of reasonably good mind and reasonably sound training, to be misled by the false and diseased philosophy which has produced them? Internationalism seems an alluring pose to many a clever young college fellow. But it is a pose which, if persevered in, means that the man loses all power of aiding in the development of a really vigorous and therefore a really national civilization.

Fundamentally, as the world now is, promiscuity in patriotism is as unwholesome as promiscuity in domestic relations. The best world-citizen is the man who is first and foremost a good citizen of his own country. Within our national limits I distrust any man who is as fond of a stranger as he is of his own family; and in international matters I even more keenly distrust the man who cares for other nations as much as for his own. I do not trust persons whose affections are so diffuse. There are men who look upon their wives or mothers or countries and upon other women and other countries with the same tepid equality of emotion. I do not regard these men as noble or broad-minded. I regard them as rotten.

This great war has offered the supreme test of the only kind of internationalism worth talking about, the sound internationalism which implies power and courage and disinterested willingness to sacrifice much in order to put down international wrong and establish international right. When the emergency test was thus applied the professional internationalists showed themselves a sorry crew. The really powerful men of intrigue and action who professed adherence to the doctrine have been the efficient and evil tools of German autocracy, militarism, and international tyranny. The milk-and-water intellectuals who prattled about the doctrine have been the timid and inefficient tools of the same foul masters.

The great war for international right and justice has been carried on by the men who were nationalists first, patriots first, Frenchmen or Englishmen or Italians or Americans first; and who were able to serve humanity at large precisely because they possessed the soul qualities which made them proudly devoted to their own nations, and proud to fight for their devotion. At this moment the menace of a peace which will consecrate German wrongdoing comes mainly from men who profess a wordy internationalism. It is the sound nationalists, the ardent patriots of the United States and of the free countries of western Europe, who are too proud not to fight to the end for Belgium and Servia and all the small well-behaved nations who are primarily threatened by the German horror.

The cultivated American, the college-bred American, the American intellectual who professes the creed of internationalism has turned

down the path that leads to moral emascula-
tion. He has given adhesion to those half-
truths that are the most destructive of false-
hoods; and these half-truths eat out the moral
fibre of mankind as plague-germs eat out the
healthy tissue of the physical body. He prac-
tises a philosophy dear to those who think idly,
dear to those who live vapidly, dear to those
whose hearts are both cold and feeble.

Let us remember this when the peace comes.
Don't trust the pacifists; they are the enemies
of righteousness. Don't trust the professional
internationalists; they are the enemies of nationalism and Americanism. Both of these
groups appeal to all weaklings, illusionists,
materialists, lukewarm Americans, and fad-
dists of all the types that vitiate sound nationalism. Their leaders are plausible make-
believe humanitarians, who crave a notoriety
that flatters their own egotism, who often
mislead amiable and well-meaning but short-
sighted persons, who care for their own worthless carcasses too much to go anywhere near
the front when fighting comes, but who in times
of inert and slothful thinking, when war seems
a remote possibility, can gain reputation by

windy schemes which imply not the smallest self-sacrifice or service among those who advocate them, and which therefore appeal to all exponents of intellectual vagary, sentimental instability and eccentricity, and that sham altruism which seeks the cheap glory of words that betray deeds. All these elements combined may, when the people as a whole are not fully awake, betray this country into a course of folly for which when the hour of stern trial comes our bravest men will pay with blood and our bravest women with tears. For these illusionists do not pay with their own bodies for the dreadful errors into which they have led a nation. They strut through their time of triumph in the hours of ease, and when the hours of trial come they scatter instantly and let the nationalists, the old-fashioned patriots, the men and women who believe in the virile fighting virtues, accept the burden and carry the load, meet the dangers and make the sacrifices, and give themselves to and for the country. Nations are made, defended, and preserved, not by the illusionists, but by the men and women who practise the homely virtues in time of peace, and who in time of righteous war are ready to die, or to send those they love best to die, for a shining ideal.

This war, into which we helplessly drifted without preparation, and in which for the first year and a quarter we did so lamentably ill, nevertheless may mean the moral salvation of our people. It has lifted us out of the stew of sordid materialism, flavored with sham sentimentality. It has brought us face to face with the eternal verities which were manfully faced by our fathers in the days of Lincoln, by our forefathers in the days of Washington. It has taught us again to realize the worth of the great basic virtues, the fundamental virtues of manhood and womanhood, which enabled Washington and Lincoln and the men of Valley Forge and the men of Gettysburg to build and to maintain this republic as the hope of the free nations of mankind. Those men were not internationalists. They were Americans. That is why we are proud to be their fellow countrymen. That is why they have been an inspiration to the best men of all other nations.

There is no limit to the greatness of the future before America, before our beloved land. But we can realize it only if we are Americans, if we are nationalists, with all the fervor of our hearts and all the wisdom of our brains. We can serve the world at all only if we serve America first and best. We must work along our own national lines in every field of achievement. We must feel in the very marrow of our being that our loyalty is due only to America, and that it is not diluted by loyalty for any other nation or all other nations on the face of the earth. Only thus shall we fit ourselves really to serve other nations, to refuse ourselves to wrong them, and to refuse to let them do wrong or suffer wrong.

CHAPTER VI

THE GERMAN HORROR

THE Germans have themselves coined the words by which to describe and denounce their conduct in this war. These are the words Schrecklichkeit and Kultur. They use the word Schrecklichkeit accurately in telling of their deeds. Its literal translation is Horror. Kultur as used by them has become a term of derision for the outside world. It can be translated as culture only in a pathological sense. German "Kultur" is precisely analogous to a "culture" of cholera-germs.

It sounds well, for the moment, to say that we war against the German Government but love the German people. Yet the antithesis thus drawn is misleading, and the effect of the statement is mischievous. It plays into the hands of the pro-Germans and pacifists, who at once ask: "Then why fight people we love?" Such a question is difficult to answer;

and inasmuch as our going to war can be justified only—although amply—by admitting that
we ought to have gone to war two years previously, it is unwise to furnish further ammunition to the foolish or sinister creatures who
seek to embarrass the government by asking
why we now make war for causes which during
two years and a half we were told did not justify
war.

Moreover, the statement, in addition to
being unwise, is untrue. There is no such difference between the German Government and
the German people as is implied. Unques-
tionably the hideous wrong-doing of the German Government to-day would have struck
with horror and amazement the German people
of fifty years ago—still more the men of '48,
who had faith in the vision of justice and mercy.
But the scientific, efficient, and utterly ruthless
and conscienceless administration which Prussia under the Hohenzollerns has imposed on
all Germany during the last half-century has
completely debauched the German people.

We must remember that serfage did not come
to an end in Germany until as a sequel to the
wars of Napoleon. The constitution of Prus-

sian society is aristocratic, capitalistic, and militaristic to the core, and the guiding and ruling minority of this society has for a couple of centuries been saturated with the spirit of cynical and faithless brutality. It was this ruling minority which, after using for its own end the Tugendbund, and the self-sacrificing idealism of the German popular revolt against Napoleon, instantly betrayed its liberty-loving supporters when once Napoleon was overthrown.

Unfortunately for Germany, of the German leaders of the mid-nineteenth century those who were liberal were pacifist and impractical, and they could not make headway against the selfish and brutal but severely practical genius of the men who followed Bismarck. The very docility of the German masses, long accustomed to being ruled, made them easy victims of the domineering, materialistic, hard-headed and coarse-tempered upper classes who rose to the surface as Germany became Prussianized. The autocracy was victorious at home and abroad; its rule was ruinous to the souls of the people, but it shrewdly took care of their bodies; and it completely subdued them to its will. By degrees the intellectuals became as repulsively indifferent to all morality that was not strictly tribal as the militarists themselves; and the masses blindly followed suit.

The attitude of the professors and literary men in this war has been as abhorrent, as utterly vile, as that of the brutes in uniform who have planned and carried out the wholesale murders, the obscene and loathsome cruelties and devastations, the huge slave-raids, and the carnivals of destruction in the conquered lands. The bombing of American hospitals and submarining of Canadian hospital-ships are merely minor instances of what has been done. And the people as a whole have applauded the infamies committed and have enthusiastically supported the authors of these infamies.

In nations as in men there is apt to be a mixture of the Dr. Jekyll and the Mr. Hyde; and able leaders, according to the degree in which conscience and wisdom guide their ability, bring to the fore one or the other type of national characteristic. For half a century in Germany as a whole, and for a much longer time in Prussia, the effective national leadership has been such as to develop efficiency on

a basis as fundamentally immoral, both from
the international and the democratic stand-
points, as that of ancient Assyria herself. The
conscience of the German people has been
thoroughly debauched. In consequence the
German people now stand behind their government and heartily support it in every infamy
it commits. The greatest good fortune that
could befall the German people would be the
crushing defeat of Germany. Until such a
defeat occurs we can only say that, unless the
German people separate themselves from and
condemn and repudiate, instead of upholding,
the German Government, all right-minded and
courageous men must include them in a common condemnation.

Many of our politicians are pavidly fearful
of admitting this obvious fact lest they offend
the "German vote." Political expediency is
right enough in its place; but not when it con-
flicts with vital national interest. Our people
are not to be excused if they fail now to insist
that the day for temporizing with avowedly
foreign "votes" has passed. We have in this
country room only for thoroughgoing Americans. We care not where the man's parents

are from or where he himself was born, or what religion he professes, so long as he is in good faith and without reservation an American and nothing else. But if he tries to be half American and half something else, it is proof positive that he isn't an American at all and the sooner he gets out of the country the better. Some of the German-American papers who fear to commit treason by openly championing "Deutschland," Germany, now try to compromise by preaching devotion to "Deutschtum," that is, Germanism. This really represents no improvement. Germanism here at home is the foe of Americanism and those who believe in it should go back to Germany, where they belong. Germanism abroad is the foe not only of America but of all free and self-respecting nations. The hideous iniquities committed by Germany during the present war have been deliberately ordered by the German Government as part of its deliberate campaign of "Schrecklichkeit," of horror. They are not sporadic, they are systematic. Because of them Germany has earned the loathing felt only for criminals of utterly debased type. Vernon Kellogg, an eye-witness, in an

Atlantic Monthly article, has shown that the German people stand behind their government and share its dreadful guilt.

CHAPTER VII

SERVICE AND SELF-RESPECT

UNLESS democracy is based on the principle of service by everybody who claims the enjoyment of any right, it is not true democracy at all. The man who refuses to render, or is ashamed to render, the necessary service is not fit to live in a democracy. And the man who demands from another a service which he himself would esteem it dishonorable or unbecoming to render is to that extent not a true democrat. No man has a right to demand a service which he does not regard as honorable to render; nor has he a right to demand it unless he pays for it in some way, *the payment to include respect for the man who renders it.* Democracy must mean mutuality of service rendered, and of respect for the service rendered.

A leading Russian revolutionist (who is, of course, like every true friend of freedom, an opponent of the Bolsheviki) recently came to

this country from Vladivostock. He traversed
the Siberian railway. The porter on his train
refused to get him hot water or to black his
boots; stating with true Bolshevistic logic that
democracy meant that nobody must do anything for any one else and that anyhow his
union would turn him out if he rendered such
service.

Now, this Bolsheviki porter was foolish
with a folly that can only be induced by pro-
longed and excessive indulgence in Bolshevism or some American analogue. But the
root trouble in producing his folly was the
fact that under the old system the men whose
boots the porter blacked looked down on him
for blacking them. Are we entirely free from
this attitude in America? Until we are we
may as well make up our minds that to just
that extent we are providing for the growth
of Bolshevism here. No man has a right
to ask or accept any service unless under
changed conditions he would feel that he could
keep his entire self-respect while rendering it.
Service which carries with it the slightest im-
plication of social abasement should not be
rendered.

For a number of years I lived on a ranch in the old-time cattle country; and I also visited at the house of a backwoods lumberjack friend. In both places we lived under old-style American conditions. We all of us worked, and our social distinctions were essentially based on individual worth. We accepted as a matter of course that the difference in degree of service rendered ought at least roughly to correspond to the difference in reward. Each did most of the purely personal things for himself. But nobody thought of any necessary work as degrading.

I remember that once, when there was a lull in outdoor work, I endeavored to be useful in and around the house. I fed the pigs; and on an idle morning I blacked all the boots. Ordinarily our boots did not need blacking—most of them were not that kind. On this occasion I started, with an enthusiasm that outran my judgment, to black the dress boots of every one, of both sexes. I coated them with a thick, dull paste; only a few knobs became shiny; and the paste came off freely on what it touched. As a result I temporarily lost not merely the respect but even the affection of all the other inmates of the house. However, I did not lose caste because I had blacked the boots. I lost caste because I had blacked them badly. But I was allowed to continue feeding the pigs. The pigs were not so particular as the humans.

Now, there is no more reason for refusing to bring hot water or black boots or serve a dinner or make up a bed or cook or wash clothes (I have cooked and washed clothes often—but neither wisely nor well) than for refusing to shoe a horse, run a motor, brake a train, sell carpets, manage a bank, or run a farm. A few centuries back men of good lineage felt that they lost caste if they were in trade or finance—in some countries they feel so to this day. In most civilized lands, however, the feeling has disappeared, and it never occurs to any one to look down on any one else because he sells things. Just the same feeling should obtain, and as we grow more civilized will obtain, about all other kinds of service. This applies to domestic service. It is as entirely right to employ housemaids, cooks, and gardeners as to employ lawyers, bankers, and business men or cashiers, factory-hands, and stenographers.

But only on condition that we show the same respect to the individuals in one case as in the other cases!

Ultimately I hope that this respect will show itself in the forms of address, in the courtesy titles used, as well as the consideration shown, and the personal liberty expected and accorded. I am not demanding an instant change—I believe in evolution rather than revolution. But I am sure the change is possible and desirable; and even although it would be foolish and undesirable to set up the entirely new standard immediately, I hope we can work toward it. One of the most charming gentlewomen I know, the wife of a man of rare cultivation, ability, and public achievement, lives on the top floor of a tenement-house in a Western city. The rooms are comfortably and daintily furnished— with an abundance of books. In this household the maid was introduced to me as Miss So-and-So; and this is the ideal. Of course it cannot be realized until there has been much education *on both sides*. But it should be the ideal. All relations between employer and employee should be based on mutuality of respect and consideration; arrogance met by insolence, or an alternation of arrogance and insolence, offers but a poor substitute.

Mutuality of respect and consideration, service and a reward corresponding as nearly as may be to the service—these make up the ideal of democracy. Such an ideal is as far from the stupid bourbonism of reaction as it is from the vicious lunacy of the Bolsheviki or I. W. W. type. Perhaps the beginning of its realization may come through the introduction of universal military training. Some months ago I went through the National Army, or drafted men's, camp at Chillicothe, Ohio. There were some thirty thousand men in the camp—Americans of fine type, who were having the finest kind of education, for these camps are the true universities of American citizenship. An exceptionally efficient and far-seeing army officer, Major-General Glenn, was in command. He kept admirable discipline, he tolerated no slackness, no failure in duty of any kind, and by his initiative and personality he was overcoming all obstacles and making capital soldiers of his men. He showed with especial pride the Red Cross Community House. It is a huge building, very attractive, with a big restaurant, reading-rooms, and a dance-hall. When off duty officers and enlisted men come there and bring their friends of both sexes, with absolutely no restriction save, as General Glenn put it, that "every man is to act as a gentleman and every woman as a gentlewoman." (When we have universal service, and every man has served in the ranks, and representatives of every class have commissions, there will be merely the same distinction between sergeants and lieutenants as between captains and colonels.) In the restaurant the major-general and a private from the ranks may—and sometimes do—sit at the same table. All come alike to the dances. All alike enjoy the privileges of the reading-rooms. All behave with self-respect. Each respects the others. When they go back to duty each does his allotted task in his allotted position, with eager and zealous efficiency, and with alert, orderly, and instant discipline. Surely this is the military ideal for a democracy— twenty years ago my own regiment realized just this ideal. Surely it also represents substantially the democratic ideal toward which we should strive in civil life. It is as far removed from the brutal and repulsive folly of Bolshevism on the one hand as from the intolerable autocratic tyranny of the Hohenzollern type on the other.

CHAPTER VIII

THE ROMANOFF SCYLLA AND THE BOLSHEVIST CHARYBDIS

FROM the days when civilized man first began to strive for self-government and democracy success in this effort has depended primarily upon the ability to steer clear of extremes. For almost its entire length the course lies between Scylla and Charybdis; and the heated extremists who insist upon avoiding only one gulf of destruction invariably land in the other—and then take refuge in the meagre consolation afforded by denouncing as "inconsistent" the pilot who strives to avoid both. Throughout past history Liberty has always walked between the twin terrors of Tyranny and Anarchy. They have stalked like wolves beside her, with murder in their red eyes, ever ready to tear each other's throats, but even more ready to rend in sunder Liberty herself. Always in the past there has been a monotonously recurrent cycle in the history of free states; Liberty has supplanted Tyranny, has gradually been supplanted by Anarchy, and has then seen the insupportable Anarchy finally overthrown and Tyranny re-established. Anarchy is always and everywhere the handmaiden of Tyranny and Liberty's deadliest foe. No people can permanently remain free unless it possesses the stern self-control and resolution necessary to put down anarchy. Order without liberty and liberty without order are equally destructive; special privilege for the few and special privilege for the many are alike profoundly anti-social; the fact that unlimited individualism is ruinous, in no way alters the fact that absolute state ownership and regimentation spells ruin of a different kind. All of this ought to be trite to reasonably intelligent people—even if they are professional intellectuals—but in practice an endless insistence on these simple fundamental truths is endlessly necessary.

Before our eyes the unfortunate Russian nation furnishes an example on a gigantic scale of what to avoid in oscillating between extremes. The autocratic and bureaucratic despotism of the Romanoffs combined extreme tyranny with extreme inefficiency; and the Bolshevists have turned the revolution into a veritable Witches' Sabbath of anarchy, plunder, murder, utterly faithless treachery and inefficiency carried to the verge of complete disintegration. Each side sought salvation by formulas which were condemned alike by common sense and common morality; and even these formulas were by their actions belied.

I do not say these things from any desire to speak ill of the Russian people. I am far too conscious of our own smug shortcoming during the world war to wish to comment harshly on a great people which has suffered terribly and which battled bravely for the three years during which we as a nation earned the curse of Meroz by the complacent and greedy selfishness with which we refused to come to the help of the Lord against the mighty—while our leaders with unctuous hypocrisy justified our course by deliberate falsehood and by a sham sentimentality which under the circumstances was nauseous. Our astute profiting by the valor of others saved us from paying the terrible penalty which Russia has paid; but from the standpoint of national and international morality our offense was well-nigh as rank as Russia's. Since the Bolshevists rose to power Russia has betrayed her own honor and the cause of world democracy, and the liberties of well-behaved minorities within her own borders, and the right to liberty and self-government of small, well-behaved nations everywhere. But for the two years after the *Lusitania* was sunk, we continued to fawn on the blood-stained murderers of our people, we were false to ourselves and we were false to the cause of right and of liberty and democracy throughout the world. Had we done our duty when the *Lusitania* was sunk, instead of following the advice of the apostles of greedy and peaceable infamy, the world war with its dreadful slaughter would long ago have been over. Incidentally Russia would have been saved from the abyss into which she has fallen, for in her inevitable revolution the Bolshevists would not have had the German support which has enabled them to wrench loose the very foundations of their country. No wonder poor Kerensky during his brief and perilous moment of leadership exclaimed that it was America's turn to do the

fighting and endure the loss, for the three years'
effort had strained Russia to the snapping-
point.

Moreover, we can feel genuine sympathy
with the immense mass of Russian peasants,
who have never been given the chance to learn
self-government or to discriminate between
possibilities and impossibilities, and who in
their ignorance and poverty, their suffering
and bewilderment must not be too heavily
blamed for behaving as, when all is said, a
very considerable fraction of our own people
were anxious to behave. And during the last
year or eighteen months our own government
has behaved toward Russia with such short-
sightedness and infirmity of purpose, such
failure to adopt either or any of the possible
courses until it was too late to get more than
a fraction of the possible benefit, that it behooves us to be very charitable in our estimate
of the Russian people. We did not give the
Soviet governments the peaceful economic
aid they asked, nor promise them military aid
against Germany when it seemed likely that
they would accept it. Yet we did not back
the Czecho-Slovaks by putting a substantial

army in Siberia early last spring. We ought then to have put at least fifty thousand of our troops, under Leonard Wood, into Siberia; and had we done so the battle-front would now have been between the Urals and Moscow. But our government wabbled and hesitated, finally sent a few thousand men, promised aid to the Czecho-Slovaks, and then said that after all we must not go as far west as the Urals. We failed to put into Siberia a force comparable in size, and therefore in military efficiency, with the force put in by the Japanese; and we let the Japanese surpass us in military credit with the Siberian people and in laying the foundation for future economic relations with Siberia. We incurred the bitter hostility of the Soviet leaders; but we rendered very little real help to any one. We broke the peace; but we only went to war a little. We were neither wise and generous friends nor just and fearless foes. We never acted until after the best time for action had passed. We hit; but we hit softly.

Some part of the horror of famine and disease which now lies like a nightmare on the Russian people is due to our own failure to render efficient aid along any line in the past. This horror will grow worse during the winter that is opening; and surely it is our duty with generous and open-handed wisdom to bend every effort to sending help at the earliest possible moment to the starving Russian people.

It is absolutely imperative for the sake of this nation that we shall realize the lamentable calamities that have befallen Russia and shall condemn in sternest fashion the men in our own country who would invite such calamities for America. The reactionaries, the men whose only idea is to restore their power to the bourbons of wealth and politics, and obstinately to oppose all rational forward movements for the general betterment, would, if they had their way, bring to this country the ruin wrought by the régime of the Romanoffs in Russia. To withstand the sane movement for social and industrial justice is enormously to increase the likelihood that the movement will be turned into insane and sinister channels. And to oscillate between the sheer brutal greed of the haves and the sheer brutal greed of the have-nots means to plumb the depths of degradation. The soldiers who in this war have battled at the front against autocracy will not submit to the enthronement of privilege at home. They believe in discipline and leadership, they believe in the superior reward going to leaders like General Pershing and Admiral Sims; but they believe that in time the difference in industrial reward between the good man at the top of the management class and the good man in the working man's class ought roughly to correspond to the difference in reward between the general and the sergeant-major, the admiral and the warrant-officer.

We will not submit to privilege in the form of wealth. Just as little will we submit to the privilege of a mob. There are no worse enemies of America than the American Bolshevists and the crew of politicians who pander to them. We ought therefore clearly to understand what the Bolsheviki attempted in Russia and what after a year of power they have done for, or rather to, Russia. They utterly repudiated the idea of a democracy, where every man is guaranteed his rights and is limited in his power to do wrong. Their effort was to create a Marxian socialistic state, based on the class-conscious purpose of the proletariat to

destroy and rob every other class. They oppressed and plundered impartially all former
oppressors and wrong-doers and all former
champions of fair dealing and liberty. They
attacked the erstwhile corrupt bureaucrat
or wealthy landowner who had neglected all
his duties not a whit more venomously than
they attacked the small shopkeeper or skilled
mechanic or industrious farmer or thrifty
working man whom, because he had saved some
money and began to live decently, they denounced as having adopted "bourgeois standards." They definitely sought to realize the
stark formulas of Marxian socialism; and therefore they have made a genuine contribution for
warning and prevention against destructive
adventure of a similar character in our own
land. The followers of Trotzky and Lenine,
like the followers of Robespierre and Marat,
have just one lesson to teach the American
people: what to avoid.

In the peace treaty of last March the Russian
Bolshevists and the German autocracy joined
against the free nations. Anarchy and despotism joined against liberty. The representatives of the privilege of a proletarian mob and

the representatives of the privilege of a pluto-
cratic oligarchy struck hands against the men
who believe in no privilege. Germany suppressed Bolshevism and restored military order
in the Russian provinces the Bolshevists ceded
to her, and cynically supported Bolshevism
in the rest of Russia precisely because Bolshevism is a cancerous growth; Germany
recognizes that anarchy destroys freedom;
therefore Germany encourages anarchy in every
land to which she cannot apply her own iron
despotism; for she wishes to destroy every nation that she cannot enslave. The Bolshevist
leaders—it matters not whether they were
sinister visionaries or the corrupted agents of
Germany—played Germany's game in order
to gain a respite during which they brought still
further destruction to their own countrymen.
They preached socialism and practised anarchy
—in their extreme forms the two always meet
when the effort is made actually to apply them.

Surely this lesson will not be lost on the
people of the United States, the keen, kindly,
brave people, who are often slow to wake but
who are far-sighted and resolute when once
awake. We of the United States must set

ourselves to the task of ordering our own household in the spirit of Abraham Lincoln. Therefore we must realize that the reactionaries among us are the worst foes of order, and the revolutionaries the worst foes of liberty; and unless we can preserve both order and liberty the republic is doomed. At the moment the profiteers, and all men who make fortunes out of this war, represent the worst types of reactionary privilege; and on a level of evil with them stand all the various exponents of American Bolshevism. Prominent, although not always powerful, among the latter are the professional intellectuals, who vary from the soft-handed, noisily self-assertive frequenters of frowsy restaurants to the sissy socialists, the pink-tea and parlor Bolshevists, who support what they regard as "advanced" papers, and aspire to notoriety as make-believe "reds." I call these persons "intellectuals" in deference to the terminology of European politics; for they ape the silly, half-educated people, and the educated able people with a moral or mental twist, who in almost every European country have found notoriety and excitement in fomenting revolutionary movements which they were utterly powerless to direct or control. Unless the term intellectual is to be construed as excluding either character or common sense, it can be applied to them only in irony. In our own vernacular they have been styled the exponents of "Highbrow" Hearstism or Bolshevism. The sincere and well-meaning among them come in the class of those described by Don Marquis in his account of "Hermione and her little group of serious thinkers." Those in this class usually furnish the funds with which their more astute brethren carry on the propaganda and earn a shifty livelihood. Worthy soft-headed persons of both sexes— including some who edit magazines or write for them—think it smart and uplifting to describe with sympathy the Russian exile who wishes to smash our government because the "bourgeoisie" who love music can purchase reserved seats at a musical performance—I suppose they should be kept free for the "proletariat" to sit in ten at a time; or to eulogize the red-flag leaders of a "picnic of socialist locals" whose "spiritually alive" faces, inflamed with "explosive ideas, big emotions, and winged visions" the particular member of

Hermione's group of serious thinkers who chronicled them—and who evidently had not exercised the infinitesimal amount of thought necessary to realize just what these same explosive ideas of the red-flag gentry were at that moment producing in Russia.

I am referring to two articles chosen almost at random from respectable magazines. They represent a fad—a fad which is chiefly foolish, but which may become mischievous. The dilettante reds who gratify their vanity by this fad, play into the hands of the genuine reds, who are not dilettantes, and who resort to bomb-throwing, arson, robbery, and murder as a business and not as a fad. The leaders of the Germanized socialists of this country are traitors to America and to mankind just exactly as are the Bolshevist leaders in Russia; and some at least of the leaders of the Non-Partisan League stand on the same footing. The leaders of the I. W. W. are no more victims of social wrong, are no more protesters against social evil, than are so many professional gunmen. There are plenty of honest, misled men among the rank and file of all these organizations; and plenty of wrongs from which these men suffer; but these men can be helped, and these wrongs remedied, only if we set our faces like flint against the evil leaders who would hurl our social organism into just such an abyss as that which has engulfed Russia.

So much for the false friends of liberty. We must equally abhor the false friends of order. Those who invoke order to prevent the righting of wrong are the ultimate friends of disorder. Our sternest effort should be exerted against the man of wealth and power who gets the wealth by harming others and uses the power without regard to the general welfare. In times ahead we must avoid equally both hardness of heart and softness of head. We must substitute the full performance of duty in a brotherly spirit, both for the mean and arrogant greed of the haves and for the mean and envious greed of the have-nots. At present Germany is dangerous as a huge man-eating beast is dangerous; Russia is dangerous as an infected and plague-stricken body is dangerous. We must guard against both. And within our own borders we must steer our great free republic as far from the Romanoff Scylla as from the Bolshevist Charybdis.

I take Russia as an example of what to avoid merely because the lesson taught by Russia is vivid in the eyes of our people. Exactly the same lesson can be learned from the French Revolution of a century and a quarter ago. What I say now I said in March, 1912, at Carnegie Hall:

I prefer to work with moderate, with rational conservatives, provided only that they do in good faith strive forward toward the light. But when they halt and turn their backs to the light, and sit with the scorners on the seats of reaction, then I must part company with them. We, the people, cannot turn back. Our aim must be steady, wise progress. It would be well if our people would study the history of a sister republic. All the woes of France for a century and a quarter have been due to the folly of her people in splitting into the two camps of unreasonable conservatism and unreasonable radicalism. Had pre-revolutionary France listened to men like Turgot, and backed them up, all would have gone well. But the beneficiaries of privilege, the Bourbon reactionaries, the short-sighted ultraconservatives turned down Turgot, and then found that, instead of him, they had obtained Robespierre. They gained twenty years' freedom from all restraint and reform, at the cost of the whirlwind of the red terror; and in their turn the unbridled extremists of the terror induced a blind reaction; and so with convulsion and oscillation from one extreme to another, with alternatives of violent radicalism and violent Bourbonism, the French people went through misery toward a shattered goal. May we profit by the experiences of our brother republicans across the water, and go forward steadily, avoiding all wild extremes; and may our ultraconservatives remember that the rule of the Bourbons brought on the Revolution; and may our would-be revolutionaries remember that no Bourbon was ever such a dangerous enemy of the people and of freedom as the professed friend of both, Robespierre. There is no danger of a revolution in this country, but there is grave discontent and unrest, and in order to remove them there is need of all the wisdom and probity and deep-seated faith in and purpose to uplift humanity we have at our command.

Friends, our task as Americans is to strive for social and industrial justice, achieved through the genuine rule of the people. This is our end, our purpose. The methods for achieving the end are merely expedients to be finally accepted or rejected according as actual experience shows that they work well or ill. But in our hearts we must have this lofty purpose, and we must strive for it in all earnestness and sincerity, or our work will come to nothing. In order to succeed we need leaders of inspired idealism, leaders to whom are granted great visions, who dream greatly and strive to make their dreams come true; who can kindle the people with the fire from their own burning souls. The leader for the time being, whoever he may be, is but an instrument to be used until broken, and then to be cast aside; and if he is worth his salt he will care no more when he is broken than a soldier cares when he is sent where his life is forfeit in order that the victory may be won. In the long fight for right-eousness the watchword for us all is "spend and be spent." It is of little matter whether any one man fails or succeeds; but the cause shall not fail, for it is the cause of mankind.

We here in America hold in our hands the hope of the world, the fate of the coming years; and shame and disgrace will be ours if in our eyes the light of high resolve is dimmed, if we trail in the dust the golden hopes of men. If on this new con-tinent we merely build another country of great but unjustly divided material prosperity, we shall have done nothing; and we shall do as little if we merely set the greed of envy against the greed of arrogance, and thereby destroy the material well-being of all of us. To turn this government either into government by a plutocracy or government by a mob would be to repeat on a larger scale the lamentable failures of the world that is dead. We stand against all tyranny by the few or by the many. We stand for the rule of the many in the interest of all of us, for the rule of the many in a spirit of courage, of common sense, of high purpose, above all in a spirit of kindly justice toward every man and every woman. We not merely admit but insist that there must be self-control on the part of the people, that they must keenly perceive their own duties as well as the rights of others; but we also insist that the people can do nothing, unless they not merely have, but exercise to the full, their own rights. The worth of our great experiment depends upon its being in good faith an experiment— the first that has ever been tried—in true democracy on the scale of a continent, on a scale as vast as that of the mightiest empires of the Old World. Surely this is a noble ideal, an ideal for which it is worth while to strive, an ideal for which at need it is worth while to sacrifice much; for our ideal is the rule of all the people in a spirit of friendliest brotherhood toward each and every one of the people.

CHAPTER IX

PARLOR BOLSHEVISM

THE most powerful indictment of the corrupt and inefficient tyranny of the Romanoffs, or rather of the Russian autocracy, is that it produced Bolshevism. Dreadful though it is that despotism should ruin men's bodies, it is worse that it should ruin men's souls. Vast physical distress was caused by the centuries of despotism which Russia owed to the fact that six hundred years ago she lacked military ability to repel the Mongol warriors. But this is overweighed by the dreadful qualities of soul which the despotism produced in those who suffered under it.

We in America have a direct interest in this evil phenomenon. From the tyranny in Russia great numbers of Russians fled hither. Many of these—Mary Antin is a type—were eminently fit to live in a land which, with all its faults, is a land of freedom and of opportunity; and these gave much to the land which gave them so much. But many have been merely sources of poisonous corruption to the nation which gave them an asylum. Many of the Bolshevist exiles to this land returned to Russia when the revolution broke out, and most of these were filled with venom for this country. The prime cause lay not in our shortcomings— many though these are—but in their own corroded souls. This moral corrosion made them preach and practise the gospel of hatred and malice, not only toward all men of wealth whether they did good or evil, but toward all honest, hardworking, decent-living men and women who were not consumed by mean envy of others.

These Russian exiles were not asked to come here. They came here so as to be free from persecution and to better themselves. They owe this country everything. But the only emotions aroused in the Bolshevist type are mean hatred, mean desire to slander, and a self-pity both mean and morbid. The moral and mental attitude it introduces into this country is much more permanently mischievous than the bubonic plague, and against it we should erect a far more rigorous quarantine.

The oppressed of other lands who have developed this kind of character should be kept out of this land at all hazards; and our immigration laws should promptly be changed accordingly. There are plenty of sordid and arrogant capitalists in this land; but their most harmful and unlovely traits are no worse and no more dangerous than those of this particular type of professional proletarian. In its full development it produces the Lenines and Trotzkys who have brought Russia to the brink of the abyss, and the Hillquits and Victor Bergers and Eastmans who would lead our people into a complete ruin, of which one item would be subjection to the German autocracy. The most sordid capitalists and reactionaries can do no more harm to this country than these men, if given power, would do. The worst bourbons of politics and business stand no lower than these leaders of the American Bolshevists, of the I. W. W., the Germanized socialists, the anarchists, and all the squalid crew who preach the gospel of envy and hatred, who preach a class war which, when preaching is translated into action, expresses itself through the bomb and the torch.

These men are encouraged, and our own moral fibre is weakened, by the parlor or pink-tea or sissy Bolshevism dear to the hearts of so many of our people who like to think of themselves as intellectuals, and who are, perhaps, particularly apt to find expression for their views in the *New Republic*.[1] Most certainly, hard indifference to the conditions and opportunities of the immigrant is a hideous wrong; but it is not bettered by a dilettante sentimentalism on behalf of those among the immigrants who are of semicriminal type, whether or not they seek to mask their depravity by claiming to be the victims of social oppression. We must never again view the

[1] The natural sympathy of Germanism for Bolshevism—whether the gutter Bolshevism beloved by the Hearst publications, or the parlor Bolshevism inculcated by the *New Republic*—was incidentally and amusingly brought out by Assistant Attorney-General Becker in the course of an investigation among the interned enemy aliens at Fort Oglethorpe. One German testified that the most widely read periodicals among the interned Germans were "the *Nation* of New York and the *New Republic*. . . . [The Germans] make only a few subscriptions . . . for fear that the government censor would catch on to the popularity of the *Nation* and the *New Republic*." Many of our professional intellectuals have made a contemptible showing in this war. At the "American Sociological Congress," which met in December, 1915, the speakers in large proportion seemed to be divided between those engaged in inane pacifist prattle and those engaged in downright sinister German propaganda.

immigrant merely as a labor unit. We must think of him only as a future citizen, whose children are to share with our children the heritage of this land. We must do for him everything that is right; and we must tolerate from him nothing that is wrong.

I have spoken of immigrants of Bolshevist type. As a contrast I give the story of two Americans of the best American type. Otto Rafael was born on the East Side of New York, of parents who came from Russia. While I was police commissioner my attention was attracted to him by his saving a woman and a couple of children at a fire; I found him at the Bowery branch of the Y. M. C. A., although he is himself a Jew. He came on the police force. He did not spend his time in the indulgence of hate and envy toward those who were better off. He did his work as a policeman up to the handle, and he used his salary chiefly to help out his family. He brought over one or two kinsfolk from Russia; he educated a sister; he enabled a brother to study for and become a doctor. He is now a lieutenant of police. At the same time that he entered the force an ex-man-of-war's man, who had served his time in the United States Navy, also entered the force. His name was Edward Burke; he is another American of the best type. His parents were born in Ireland. When the Spanish War came he got a holiday for six months, re-entered the navy, and served as captain of a gun. He is a hard man physically; I doubt if he can be hurt by anything that hasn't an edge to it. He is now a captain of police.

Burke and Rafael were appointed on their merits; I wanted to get the best possible men for the force, and they owed me gratitude for putting them there only to the extent that I owed them gratitude for being the kind of men I wanted. In other words, they owed me nothing. But they have chosen to remain very stanch friends, in fair weather and foul weather. When we entered the great war, both went into training to get in the division I had asked permission to raise; each fitting himself for special work—Burke handling machine-guns, while Rafael's particular line I for the moment forget. Both would have held commissions under me if I had been allowed to raise troops.

These two men represent Americanism as

opposed to Bolshevism. They did not wallow in the emotional mud-bath, which consists of one part morbid self-pity and three parts envy, hatred, and malice toward others—a mixture equally maudlin and sinister. They didn't pity themselves at all. They didn't hate others. They merely resolved to do as well as others. And they did so. They were men.

I do not mean that these two men can be taken as typical of the whole mass. They were exceptions. They had power of initiative and of leadership. It is our duty to help make conditions such that life will be fairer and easier for all, and the highways of opportunity kept more open than hitherto. But our aim can be reached by encouraging the essentially American activities and attitude shown by these two men, and not by practising parlor Bolshevism ourselves or encouraging applied and murderous Bolshevism among immigrants.

The Bolshevists have no lesson to teach America except what to avoid. They have betrayed democracy in America, England, and France. They have plunged Russia into ruin. They fatuously hoped by this betrayal of their allies to make peace with the German militaristic autocracy, and then to betray it in turn. But the Germans were just as false, cunning, and treacherous, and a thousand times more able; and having made the Bolsheviki publish themselves to the world as traitors to liberty, they have now proceeded to trample them under foot. And the Bolsheviki showed willingness only to fight their fellow Russians; they were helpless before the German invaders.

Their chief energies have been devoted to what Lenine calls "internal war." They have announced, as reported in the press, that they intend to confiscate all the property of the "small shopkeepers, more or less well-to-do peasants, and workers who have submitted to a bourgeois point of view"—that is, thrifty skilled mechanics. In other words, their hostility is now concentrated on the analogues of American farmers, small shopkeepers, carpenters, steel puddlers, engineers, trainmen, blacksmiths, clerks, deep-sea fishermen, and the like. They announced at one time (before they finally and definitely threw Russia under the German yoke) that these men and their wives were to be employed to dig trenches, presumably because they thought they were unused to this form of labor, the announcement reading: "All members of the bourgeois class, the women as well as the men, must enter these battalions under surveillance of the Red Guard and in case of resistance must be shot." No more utter tyranny existed under the Romanoffs. They purpose to stamp out of existence all the men of leadership and of special value, all the men whose activities do most to prevent the commonwealth from sinking to that level of savagery on which the tonguey, supple, and either immoral or crack-brained anarchist leaders would land their deluded followers.

The precise analogues of these Russian leaders preach similar doctrines and a similar class war here in the United States. They are permitted to do so because it is our wise principle not to interfere with free speech by prohibiting the preaching even of moral treason until the narrow limits of legal treason are reached; and our people as a whole regard them with good-humored and rather ignorant indifference. But there should be no mistake as to the fact that the preaching of this kind of class war has nothing in common with ordinary political discussion or party differences. The attempt to translate it into serious action would mean real war—and in a healthy country like ours the lunatic fringe would not come off first best in such event.   And in such event if the real Bolshevists were successful the parlor Bolshevists would be among the first to be destroyed— exactly as the Petit Trianon disciples of Rousseau were among the first to fall when the red terror swept France.   And if (as would surely happen) the real Bolshevists were not successful, the parlor Bolshevists would owe their shivering safety to the applied and practical Americanism of men like Burke and Rafael.

It is the Burkes and Rafaels and the men of like quality in every section of our country and in every walk of life, whatever their creed and whatever their ancestry, who stand for the real and practical Americanism; and it is in their hands that the future of this country lies.

CHAPTER X

TELL THE TRUTH AND SPEED UP THE WAR

OUR prime need now is, and for eighteen months has been, to speed up the war. The chief method of making the government meet this need has been telling the truth.

In handling our army and navy deeds are everything and words unbacked by deeds or betrayed by deeds are worse than nothing. When last March General Wood and General Young and Mr. Taft and the present writer asked for the immediate raising of an army of five million troops (we meant fighting soldiers, and not an alloy of 40 per cent of non-combatants), our purpose was not rhetorical. We desired to see the army provided for by law and then called into being by executive action. But to President Wilson the matter seemed primarily one of competitive rhetoric. Obviously he felt uneasy about the proposal and

treated it as one which could be deftly put
aside by adroit use of language. Accordingly,
with marked histrionic effect, he asked, "why
limit the army" to the five million we proposed, and announced that he wished an army
"without limit." This was highly satisfactory
as rhetoric. But the action of the President,
taken through his Secretary of War, showed
that it was merely rhetoric. The *phrase* was
an "army without limit"; the *fact* was that the
army was fixed at a much lower limit than that
which we had asked, and was thus fixed six
months after we urged immediate action. Secretary Baker did not set himself to meet our
greatest military need of to-day, which is a
thorough mobilization of our whole man-power
for service in our armies and in our war indus-
tries. He set himself to prevent the meeting
of this need. Congress last spring made ready
to go ahead with the "fight or work" plan.
But Mr. Baker, acting for the President, inter-
vened. He asked for delay, for procrastina-
tion, and of course thereby paralyzed congressional action. He protested against the en-
largement of the draft-age limits. He protested
against planning more than a few months in

advance. He said that we were "many months ahead of our original hope in regard to the transportation of men" overseas; but he omitted to add that this was because the original plans were hopelessly inadequate.

Never in our history has there been more fatuous incompetence than that displayed, alike in plan and action, by the War Department during the first nine months after we entered the war. Then the Military Affairs Committee of the Senate rendered the American people its debtor by stepping in and forcing some reorganization, some efficiency, in the War Department. But the Department still refused to do anything that really counted overseas. In March, when the great German drive began, a year after we had entered the war, our gallant little army in France numbered fewer soldiers (not non-combatants) than those in the army of little Belgium, and did not possess a single airplane, tank, or field-gun, save those we had obtained from the hard-pressed French. The tremendous German drive galvanized even the War Department into action. It was Ludendorff who effectively revised the plans of President Wilson and Secretary Baker.

Then the English lent us ships, and we really did begin to send men abroad, until we had perhaps a million soldiers and over half as many non-combatants across. We actually did what we ought to have done, and by the exercise of moderate efficiency would have done, just one year previously. But in June the drive for the time being halted, and immediately Mr. Baker proposed a reversion to our former Rip Van Winkle slumber. Of course, what we ought to do now is with the utmost energy to prepare to place a gigantic army overseas next year. We have begun in earnest to build ships and airplanes, and are preparing to build cannon and tanks. We are more populous and with greater resources than Germany. We are more populous than France and Great Britain combined. These nations have been through a terrible four years' war. We have as yet suffered no serious strain. Next spring we ought to have in France an army larger than the German army. We ought to have an army larger than the armies of England and France combined; we ought to have our troops fighting alongside the gallant Italian army and in the Balkans; we ought to

have one or two hundred thousand men ferried
in Japanese ships to take part in the great war
for civilization against the Turks in western
Asia; and we ought to have at least a hundred
thousand fighting troops in Siberia. This
means that we ought to have overseas next
spring an army of five million fighting men,
which in turn means that we ought to provide
now for an army of between six and seven million men all told.

Nor is it only our army as to which there is
now failure to provide for the future. The
same is true for the navy. During the first
six months of the war the navy was almost as
badly handled as the army, and it has not yet
recovered from its complete mismanagement
during the previous four years. Four years
ago Admiral Bradley Fiske dared to tell the
truth about naval conditions. He thereby rendered a very great service to the country, and
for doing this the authorities punished him,
exactly as Wood was punished for similar truth-
telling; and thereby in both cases they served
notice on the best men in the army and navy
that they jeopardized their careers if they told
the truth in the interest of our people as a

whole.   During the last nine months the navy
appears to have been on the whole well handled—and the officers and enlisted men on the
ships have made the same admirable record
that has been made by the officers and enlisted
men of our army and marine corps ashore.
Admiral Sims and those serving under him
have made all our people their debtors. But
it now also appears from the published letters
and statements of Admirals Benson and Palmer
that we are not taking thought for the future
so far as the navy is concerned. The two admirals show that we are far short of the proper
number not only of enlisted men but of officers.
Incidentally the letter of Admiral Palmer,
dated June 7, shows that the naval experts
in the Department reported to the Secretary
that we need "an enlisted strength of 225,000
men, if we are to carry on a successful war."
Mr. Daniels, however, refused to follow the
recommendations of his skilled naval advisers
and asked only for 131,000 men, which, says
Admiral Palmer, "is very much less than our
requirements to organize the navy for war,"
and the leading majority members of the House
Naval Committee opposed even this increase.

Admiral Palmer in his letter states the truth with vigorous precision, saying that the fleet and shore organizations of the navy "on paper appear to be ready for any emergency; but actually they are not. . . . To fail to recognize this situation is to court national disaster. . . . Such a weakness in the navy invites a national catastrophe. Even though, through the strength of our allies, no national catastrophe does come, it is not a wise policy to spend a billion and a half for a navy a year, and then not use it well because it costs a million more to pay the men to run it properly." Admiral Benson, in taking the same position, derides anew the argument that we need not prepare because "the war may end soon," and says that even if this fatuous statement is true, "a navy comparable with our importance is the first essential. . . . Ships alone cannot make a navy . . . it is equally essential that we have the men to man these ships and the officers of all grades sufficient to insure the efficiency of the whole."

Reading these admirable statements by trained war officers, we realize keenly the grave wrong done this nation when the administration deliberately muzzled the army officers, who before the war could and would have told our people their urgent military needs, by the following order:

WAR DEPARTMENT,
WASHINGTON, February 23, 1915.
General Orders No. 10.

Officers of the Army will refrain, until further orders, from giving out for publication any interview, statement, discussion, or article on the military situation in the United States or abroad, as any expression of their views on this subject at present is prejudicial to the best interests of the service.

[2260070, A. G. O.]

By order of the Secretary of War:

H. L. SCOTT,
Brigadier General, Chief of Staff.

By this order we deprived our people of all chance of learning from military experts our military needs. Our soldiers, the men of deeds, were forbidden to tell us how to turn our talk into deeds; and they were thus forbidden by the politicians, the men of phrases, who talked incessantly and did nothing to back up their talk.

It is well to remember that, when this order was issued, the present Secretary of War, Mr. Baker, was mayor of Cleveland; and he at about that time notified the representatives of the Security League that "he was a pacifist and was opposed to the agitation for preparedness." A year later, although President Wilson had been notified by Ambassador Gerard that Germany intended to attack America if victorious over the Allies, he appointed Mr. Baker Secretary of War. By no possibility could Mr. Wilson have rendered a greater service to the Kaiser and the German militarists.

A Russian peasant woman, Madam Botchkareva, a major in the Woman's Death Battalion, who has been wounded four times in battle with the Germans, came here from Siberia last May to beg us to help Russia with facts instead of phrases. The authorities in Washington have at each successive crisis in Russia acted from one to ten months after the action was useless. They failed to give economic help. They feared to take military action. They endeavored to conciliate the Bolshevists and yet not to do anything for them. They endeavored to oppose the pro-

German Russians, and yet not to offend them too deeply. They hoped for success in the effort, so dear to those who at heart are pacifists, to hit soft, to hit a little, but not very much. Botchkareva insisted that only an army (backed, of course, by ample economic aid for the Russians) would be of real help to Russia against the Germans and the pro-German Bolshevists, and she was outspoken in her comments on the proposal to hit soft, remarking to one of our high administrators: "You Americans seem to delight in rivers of words. I have no time for words. I want to know what you are going to do to stop Germany; and I am here to tell you one way of doing it."

Recently there have occurred several incidents which ought to wake this nation to recognition of the fact that fine phrases are no substitutes for brave deeds, and that reliance upon them represents folly.

For several years we submitted (as we are now submitting) to the murder of our citizens, the rape of our women, and finally to the killing of our soldiers, by the authorized representatives of the Mexican Government. We waged two inglorious little wars with the Mexican

Government, but finally admitted defeat and not only recognized but fawned upon those responsible for the outrages. We were told that thereby we would so impress the Mexicans with our good intentions and magnanimity and desire for peace that they would begin to love us dearly. Of course, we merely incurred their utter contempt and turned Mexico into a hot-bed of anti-American and pro-German intrigue. The results of timidity masquerading as peace-ful forbearance are set forth in a recent article in a strong administration but stanchly pa-triotic newspaper, the St. Louis *Republic*, as follows: "We have twice invaded the territory of our neighbor to the south, withdrawing each time without any very definite accomplishment except to leave a trail of bitter feeling. We now have more bitter enemies in Mexico than in any other country except Germany." If we had shown strength and courage we would have secured Mexico's genuine respect. Benev-olent phrasemongering has not proved a satis-factory substitute for strength and courage. It never will so prove. It did not so prove with Germany. If after this war we persist in it, other nations will grow to regard us as

Germany and Mexico now do. The American pacifist has been the potent ally of the German militarist and the silly tool of the Hun within our gates. In the future we shall gain the respect and friendship of well-disposed nations and the respect and fear of ill-disposed nations by prepared strength; and professions of pacifism and of general good intentions, if we fail to prepare our strength, will conciliate nobody, will make us despised by everybody, and will expose us to the hostility of the forces of evil throughout the world.

This war will not be won by phrases. It will be won by the hard fighting of the fighting men at the front. And when this war has been won, America will not be able to keep the respect or even the good-will of other nations by fine phrases about internationalism, pacifism, a League of Nations, and the like. We must trust to deeds, not words; to facts, not phrases. We must trust to an aroused, unified, and intense spirit of nationalism and to the prepared readiness to defend our rights, and the rights of others, by our own hardened strength and courage.

Everything we have accomplished in this

war—including going into the war—has been
due solely to courageous, constructive criticism
of the administration, and insistence upon
telling the truth in order to get us into the
war, and then to make us do our duty in the
war.

Only truth-telling in fearless criticism forced
our entry into the war, and forced our belated
preparedness for the war. Only resolute ham-
mering forced the raising of our army to something like a proper size, and forced its being
sent overseas. Nothing but steady criticism
and relentless exposure put a stop to the do-
nothing policy as regards ships, troops, rifles,
airplanes, machine-guns, cannon, and tanks.
Nothing but complaint and agitation brought
some improvement in the actual management
of the War Department. The moral awakening
of America, and the growth in our win-the-
war efficiency, have been due solely to the
pressure brought on the administration by
fearless truth-telling and constructive criticism
from without. Nothing has done more damage
than the persistent concealment of the facts
and denial of the truth by the administration
and its constant glittering prophecies, which

were not fulfilled. It would be well for it to remember the recent answer of Marshal Foch when asked about future prospects: "Realities are far better than any sort of promise. It is useless to make promises that may give rise to exaggerated hopes. Nothing but realities count."

CHAPTER XI

BROOMSTICK PREPAREDNESS

A STUDY of the American army for the year succeeding our entry into the war is a study of the effects of broomstick preparedness. All who defend this type of preparedness are themselves, however amicable and well-meaning, broomstick apologists. Over eighteen months have now passed since we admitted that we were at war, and over twenty months since the Germans frankly began war upon us. With our immense man-power, wealth, and resources, the natural fighting qualities of our men and the business energy and the mechanical efficiency of our people, we have now developed a force that has made us a highly important factor in the war. Seventeen months after we entered the war we at last had a sufficiency of well-trained troops to enable General Pershing for the first time to take part in the war with a separate army, an army such as the French had and the English had. But this army was still very small in size, compared to either the French or British armies. Moreover it was able to act only because it had obtained from our allies the cannon, airplanes, tanks, machine-guns, and the gas necessary in modern warfare. Without what we have thus obtained from our allies we would have been absolutely helpless. But the gallantry and fighting efficiency of our men, and the fact that several hundred thousand are now fit for use at the front, have made us already of very real weight against the Germans, for when the scales are almost trembling in the balance a relatively small weight of effort will determine the outcome. Therefore, the large number of well-meaning persons who are very forgetful, and who like to tickle their vanity by refusing to face what is unpleasant, tend already to say that our unpreparedness did not amount to anything after all, and that all things are all right, and that nobody must speak about the wrongs of the past. For this reason it is essential that our people should know just what our shortcomings were.

We cannot learn about these shortcomings from military officers. The administration by its treatment of General Wood has ren-

dered it a work of the highest danger for any
American army officer to tell the truth that
ought to be told. General Wood, two years
before we went into the war, and again one
year before we went into the war, appeared
before the Congressional Military Committees
and set forth our needs. When at the end of
last winter he returned from his stay in France,
he told us what ought at once to be done. The
administration in every case refused to profit
by what he had testified, and yet in every case
the events have made good everything he said.
It is to General Wood that we owe primarily
the Plattsburg officers' training-camps in 1915
and 1916. These Plattsburg training-camps
did a work that cannot be overestimated, in
providing officers; and it was the one really
effective bit of preparation on our part. All
that General Wood thus advised and thus did
was of the very highest value to the country.
Instead of rewarding him for it, the administration has punished him in the way hardest
to bear for a gallant and patriotic soldier. This
has represented not only a cruel injustice to
him, but a deeply unpatriotic refusal to meet
the country's needs.

Therefore, I am not at liberty to quote the first-hand testimony I have had as to some of the vital shortcomings in the administration of the War Department and the army during the first eighteen months of the war.

But in the camps I visited I saw some things so evident that no harm can come to any officer from my speaking of them; and there are some things which are now matters of common knowledge, although the War Department did everything it could to keep them from the knowledge of the people.

In the fall of 1917 the enormous majority of our men in the encampments were drilling with broomsticks or else with rudely whittled guns. As late as the beginning of December they had in the camps almost only wooden machine-guns and wooden field-cannon. In the camps I saw barrels mounted on sticks on which zealous captains were endeavoring to teach their men how to ride a horse. At that time we had one or two divisions of well-trained infantry in France—which would have been simply lapped up if placed against the army of any formidable military power. At that time, eight months after we had gone to war, the army we had gathered in the cantonments had neither the rifles, the machine-guns, the cannon, the tanks, nor the airplanes which would have enabled them to make any fight at all against any army of any military power that could have landed on our shores. It would have been as helpless against an invading army as so many savages armed with stone-headed axes. We were wholly unable to defend ourselves a year after we had gone to war. We owed our safety only to the English, French, and Italian fleets and armies.

The cause was our refusal to prepare in advance. President Wilson's message of December, 1914, in which he ridiculed those who advocated preparedness, was part of the cause. His Presidential campaign, in 1916, on the "he kept us out of war" issue was part of the cause. We paid the price later with broomstick rifles, log-wood cannon, soldiers without shoes, and epidemics of pneumonia in the camps. We are paying the price now in shortage of coal and congestion of transportation, and in the double cost of necessary war-supplies. We are paying the price and shall pay the price in the shape of taxes and a national debt at least

twice as large as would have been the case
if with forethought and wisdom we had prepared in advance. We have paid the price in
the blood of tens of thousands of gallant men.
The refusal to prepare, and the price we now
pay because of the refusal, stand in the rela-
tion of cause and effect.

I do not dwell on these facts to blame anybody. I dwell on them in order to wake our
people to the necessity of learning the lesson
they teach. In order to speed up the war it
is absolutely necessary to tell the truth. Until Senator Chamberlain's Committee on Military Affairs made its investigation there was
no change for the better in the work of the
War Department. Until Senator Thomas's
subcommittee investigated the airplane situation, the American people were kept in complete ignorance of the utter breakdown of our
air programme. Primarily this condition was
due to the policy of unpreparedness to which
the administration adhered during the two and
a half years, when even the blindest ought to
have read the lesson being taught by the great
war. Since the war broke out the administration has been guilty of numerous delays, of the

appointment and retention of inefficient men, and of many kinds of half-heartedness in waging the war. These have all caused much damage. But the prime cause was the failure to prepare in advance.

The attitude of the War Department during the first months of the war was shown by the remark of one of the high officials to the effect that the delay of a few months was "a perfectly endurable delay." This remark was made with all the complacency of the butterfly on the fence to the toad under the harrow. Others paid with their blood for our delay. The German submarine note came on January 31, 1917; and within the next two months an alert and efficient War Department would have had every particle of its programme minutely mapped out and well on the way to execution. As a matter of fact, nothing was really begun until late in August. Six months can be treated as "a perfectly endurable delay" only if we are content to accept the speed standards in war of Tiglath-Pileser and Pharaoh Nechoh. But the United States cannot afford to accept the war speed standards of the seventh century B. C., instead of those of the twentieth century, A. D. There is not the slightest use of trying to justify or excuse broomstick preparedness.

I have before me a letter from a line major of Marines, describing the terrible fighting in which the Marines took part last July. I quote the following sentences:

The German planes were thick in the air; they were in groups of from three to twenty. They would look us over and then we would soon get a pounding from their bombs. I heard men cussing as to where our $1,000,000,000 worth of planes were. We did not see them.

I also have before me a letter from an aviation major, written from another part of the front two months later, in the beginning of September. It runs in part as follows:

We still keep wondering when we are going to see the results of America's quantity efforts in aviation. Things are much better here now, but it is entirely thanks to the French. The Liberty engine has not begun to show up in quantity yet, at any rate at the front.

Every American worth his salt feels exultant pride in the splendid courage and high efficiency of our soldiers in France. From General Pershing down they have made our country, and us who dwell therein, forever their debtors.

It is well to pay these men the homage of words, but what really counts is the homage of deeds. It is a dreadful thing to send our fine and gallant boys to battle, and yet to deny them the formidable weapons and machines of war, the lack of which must be paid for by pouring out their blood like water.

As a nation we cannot be acquitted of this wrong to our fighting men whom we have sent to the front. No finer fighting men were ever known, and their deeds are deeds of deathless honor. But our government, by its failure to prepare in advance and by its delay, waste, and mismanagement after the war began, has made a record that is not pleasant for Americans to contemplate. Let our people never forget that if we had chosen to prepare in advance we would probably have ended the war in ninety days after we entered it in 1917; and that if when General Leonard Wood returned from France at the close of last winter the administration had heeded his report and had done as he then advised and as every patriotic man of knowledge and insight then hoped, we would have been further advanced at the beginning of the summer than we are now at the end of the fall. Nine-tenths of wisdom is being wise in time.

When, on February 3, we broke off diplomatic relations with Germany the war really began. From that moment avoidable, unwarranted delay was as inexcusable as it is now. The day before Mr. Elon Hooker had laid before the authorities at Washington an offer to turn over his entire plant to the service of the government, this being the plant better fitted than any other in the United States to undertake the manufacture of war gas and the development of new and more formidable kinds of gas on a gigantic scale. His request was refused. A year elapsed before any serious effort was made to undo any of the effects of the error. At the same time we had the means for building enormous quantities of excellent machine-guns. The War Department refused to avail itself of the opportunity and dallied for about eighteen months in developing a new type of gun, leaving us meanwhile without any. We dawdled in similar fashion over the tanks. We have not yet built any field-guns, and are still dependent upon what the French can give us. It is necessary merely to refer to the appalling delay in the air service where $640,000,000 were appropriated and largely expended without securing any tangible result whatever on the field of battle until we had been at war nearly a year and a half.

For nearly a year after we entered the war our authorities behaved exactly as if they believed that if they delayed long enough England and France would win the victory without us; or as if the Russian Bolshevists would disintegrate Germany; or as if in some other way, by some streak of good luck, we would be able to win the war without bloodshed, without any effort on our part. In the shipping programme and the manufacture of field-artillery, in the air programme, in the machine-gun programme, in the tank programme, in the gas programme—in short, as regards every material element necessary to win the war with the least loss of blood among the fighting men—there was the same breakdown. After a year of war, when the great German drive began, our fighting army able to take part in the active work at the front was actually smaller than that of Belgium. In the next six months we were able to place in the field an army respectable in numbers and admirable in quality; and we were able to do this only because, in view of the breakdown of our shipping programme, the British furnished their ships, so that 60 per cent of the tonnage used in ferrying our soldiers across was British. But we were able to furnish only the men. We had only the field-artillery the French furnished us. We got uniforms from the English. We did not have a single fighting-plane of American make, and naturally the French did not give us their best planes. We had very few American machine-guns or auto rifles. We had almost no gas. We had almost no tanks, and those we did have were furnished by our allies. We now have a few admirable naval guns, admirably handled, and a number of excellent bombing airplanes of our own manufacture.

The Russo-Japanese War lasted some sixteen months. During this time the Russian Government was rightly esteemed to have mismanaged matters. But the breakdown of our government for the first sixteen months after we went to war was far more complete than the breakdown of the Russian Government when opposed to Japan. At the end of that time we had some hundreds of thousands of fighting men, certainly unsurpassed, and perhaps unequalled in the world, but they had practically no artillery, tanks, airplanes, machine-guns, or gas of their own. They were still unprepared to act as an army by themselves. In other words, they would have been utterly helpless against any well-equipped modern army. After sixteen months our government had failed to meet the situation even as well as the Russian Government had met its situation. The difference was that Russia had no allies, whereas our allies made a rampart of their bodies behind which we slowly prepared.

The business efficiency of our people is great. Its man-power is great. Its resources are enormous. Had the administration, with an eye single to our country's needs, devoted its whole energy to speeding up the war, and abandoned all thought of politics during the war, the peace of overwhelming victory would by this time have been won. But this was not done. Never

before in our history has the administration
in power during a war drawn party lines as
sharply as in the present war. No one but an
active partisan adherent of the administration
has been given any position of the slightest
political responsibility; and the test in the appointment of even these, as established by
President Wilson, in his messages concerning
the election or re-election of congressmen, is
loyalty to the administration rather than loyalty to the country. But an immense number
of business men, without distinction of party—
Democrats and Republicans alike, men like
Hoover, Ryan, Stettinius, Schwab, and Hur-
ley—have come forward and rendered invalu-
able service at a nominal salary of $1 a year,
or something of the kind. Without distinction
of party our best men have gone to the front
to fight—except where, as in the case of General Wood, the administration refused to use
them. In Congress party lines have been abol-
ished on the great issues connected with waging the war efficiently. The Republicans, as a
matter of fact, furnished a greater percentage
than the Democrats of the support needed by
the President on the most important war

measures. Thanks to the work of Congress, to the work of our private citizens, and above all to the valor of our soldiers, we have been able to develop some portion of our strength; and although we are not at this time one-quarter as efficient in the war as we could have been if our leaders, without regard to politics, had devoted themselves in every way to speeding up the war, yet even the use of this small fraction of our giant strength has sufficed to turn the scale.

If we do our full duty even now, the war may be over very soon. But it may continue for a long time. In any event, let our people remember that every disaster and every delay is, will be, and has been due to our people permitting the misconduct of the men in high political position to go unrebuked. If peace comes soon—and there should be no peace permitted except the peace of complete victory, a peace secured by the unconditional surrender of Germany—let our people remember that the unfortunate individuals made the scapegoats for our numerous breakdowns were not really to blame. It is the men in highest position over them who were really to blame; and these men were most heavily to blame for their failure to prepare in advance. When President Wilson, a year after the sinking of the *Lusitania*, appointed Mr. Baker Secretary of War he absolutely insured all the trouble that has come from the breakdowns in our war programme. President Wilson has said, "We waited until every fair-minded citizen of our peace-loving democracy was aware that peace was impossible before we reluctantly began to prepare to defend ourselves"; and Secretary Baker and Mr. Creel, loyally supporting their chief, have said that they felt "delight" and "pride" in the fact that "we were not prepared." The satisfaction thus expressed and felt by the men responsible for our failure to prepare will not be shared by the mothers, the widows, and the orphans of the tens of thousands of gallant men whose deaths have been due and will be due to this failure.

If there is any lesson which this war ought to have taught it is the priceless value of time. Our delay was not fatal to us, merely because our allies protected us. Now we have begun to develop a great fighting force. No nation has finer stuff for soldiers than America; no nation has greater wealth; probably no other nation can draw on a population of such energy, administrative capacity, and inventive resourcefulness. A year after our forced entry into the war we began to become a ponderable military element; we have steadily become more and more formidable; and finally, I believe, we shall become the decisive factor in the war.

Then there will be grave danger lest our vanity mislead us into forgetfulness of our helplessness for the first year and a half, and if so we shall again sink back into a condition of utter unpreparedness. For this reason let us refuse to be guilty of the folly of keeping silent as to the facts of the two years and a half preceding and of the year and a half succeeding our entry into the war. On this matter at least it is necessary to live up to President Wilson's former desire for "pitiless publicity."

Next time we may not find allies to defend us. Let Uncle Sam prepare to defend himself. Let him realize from the experience of the immediate past that, unless he prepares long in advance, he will be utterly helpless if suddenly menaced with war by a great military nation.

Broomstick preparedness is of value only from the political standpoint.

Fine words will never save us from a foreign conqueror.   Only deeds will save us; and then only if we prepare for these deeds in advance.

Brag is a good dog.   But Holdfast is a better.

CHAPTER XII

THE GOSPEL OF SPILT MILK

THE gospel as preached nineteen hundred years ago "called sinners to repentance." The sinners who profited by it were those who repented. They did not jauntily speak of their sins as spilt milk. They recognized themselves as sinners; they recognized the need of repentance. Unless they met these three conditions, they were regarded as hypocrites (and hypocrites were not laughed at, nor excused, but scathingly denounced). If the sinners announced that they were proud of their sins or took delight in them, or if they excused themselves and denied their shortcomings, they were not regarded as having repented at all and were denied all fellowship with those who had seen the light.

And those who summoned the sinners to repent did not tell them not to cry over spilt milk. On the contrary, they told them with emphasis that they had sinned, and that there was sore need of repentance, and that such sincere repentance for the past was the surest way to strengthen their souls against future repetition of their past misconduct.

The present-day chatter against speaking the necessary truth about our past governmental misconduct is apt to find expression in a protest against "crying over spilt milk." The beneficiaries of the chatter noisily announce that they feel "pride" and "delight" in having spilled the milk in the past, instead of bending their energies in repentant silence to mopping it up in the present.

For two years and a half the world war raged and we refused to prepare. Germany trampled Belgium into bloody mire, but we refused to prepare. She sank the *Lusitania* and murdered our people wholesale upon the high seas, but we refused to prepare. She dynamited our factories at home, but we refused to prepare. Our government knew all about her plots; our governmental authorities had full knowledge of all she was doing, but they kept us ignorant and neutral and refused to prepare. Inert, timid, absorbed in money-getting, we dulled our souls with sentimental rhetoric which under such conditions was nauseous. Our leaders refused to take one thought for the terrible to-morrow or to harden a single fibre of our giant but flabby strength. We drifted into the war on a sea of fatuous phrases and fatuous refusals to act. And then for a year we waged the war with irresolute feebleness. Meanwhile the administration, through Mr. Baker, through Mr. Creel, through the President himself, have excused or denied the shortcomings, have announced that they regarded them with pride and delight and have persevered in them until dragooned out of them by hostile criticism. Yet with these facts staring us in the face, there are still persons who regard the gospel of "not crying over spilt milk" as an improvement upon the gospel of calling sinners to repentance.

It was not until the great German drive in the spring of 1918 came within a hand's breadth of wrecking the Allied cause, that our people began to wake to the actual facts, and that the administration began seriously to try to perform a substantial portion of its duty. By that time three years and nine months had passed since the great war began, and over a year had passed since Germany forced us into it.

The most terrible battle of the whole terrible war was raging, a battle which might readily have meant the winning of the war by Germany.

It was an hour of awful trial and suffering and danger for our war-worn allies who in France were battling for us no less than for themselves. If shame is ever more dreadful than suffering, then it was a no less terrible hour for our country. Our allies stood with their backs to the wall in the fight for freedom, and America looked on. The free nations stood at bay in the cause that was ours no less than theirs; and after over a year of war the army we had sent to their aid was smaller than that of poor, heroic, ruined Belgium, and was hardly more than a twentieth the size of that which gallant and impoverished Italy had in the field. And this great, wealthy nation of ours had not yet furnished to our own brave troops in the field, cannon or tanks or airplanes, and almost no machine-guns, save those which we had obtained from hard-pressed France. And let our people remember that every gun or tank or airplane thus made for us by hard-pressed France was left unmade for hard-pressed Italy.

Our few gallant fighting men overseas had even then won high honor for themselves, and had made all other Americans forever their debtors. But it was a scandal and a reproach to this nation that they were so few and so badly equipped. If in this mighty battle our allies had failed, black infamy would have been our portion, because of the delay and the folly and the weakness and the cold, time-serving timidity of our government, to which this failure would have been primarily due.

Our allies did not fail. They staved off defeat. They managed to hold until Pershing was able to put into the line seven or eight divisions sufficiently trained and of such splendid natural worth that they could be used as shock troops—although even then these troops could fight only because we had obtained from our allies the necessary cannon, airplanes, tanks, and machine-guns, and although even then we could not put in separate army corps, our troops being joined in larger or smaller units with the French or English. But the native quality of our troops was such that they were a factor of prime importance in the great counter-drive which Foch then began and which after over three months of victory, has forced Germany almost to her own borders and made her start her peace drive to avert unconditional surrender. The government is now really endeavoring to send men across the water as rapidly as possible. It is now endeavoring to speed up the ship programme. It is now endeavoring to hurry the airplane programme. It is employing big business men and apparently is giving them power. None of these things were done until Senator Chamberlain's committee in the teeth of the violent opposition of the administration, forced some efficiency and some speed into the work of war. Few of them were done effectively until the German drive galvanized the administration into action. If these obvious things and the other obvious things like them had been energetically begun a year and a half ago, the American army would now be in Germany as the dominant factor in the war. If we had begun to prepare in August, 1914, the war would have been over long ago, and indeed we probably would not have had actually to fight and an infinity of bloodshed would certainly have been spared. Verily, our own country and the world at large have paid, are paying, and will pay a heavy price for the milk spilt by the administration; and the heaviest blame rests on those false leaders of public thought who told the people not to cry over the spilt milk, instead of telling them to call the sinners to repentance and to see that the repentance was sincere and effective.

Let the sinners cease exulting over their sins and in good faith bring forth fruits meet for repentance. We are now doing what we ought to have done over a year and a half ago. We are now preparing to make our overseas army next spring what it could have been made and ought to have been made last spring. But let us not forget that the present action of the administration in increasing the army furnishes the severest condemnation of its folly last spring in refusing then to do what it is now doing, when General Wood on his return from France, and when Lieutenant-General Young and all other competent advisers insisted upon the need of instantly starting to increase our army to five million fighting men overseas.

To prepare along every line for a three years' war offers the best chance of shortening it; and if it lasts three years such preparation will guarantee us against the necessity a year hence, or two or three years hence, of trying to cover up failure by nervously assuring one another that we need not cry over spilt milk.

If those responsible for our failure, if those responsible for the refusal to prepare during the two and a half years in which we were vouchsafed such warning as never nation previously received, if those responsible for the sluggish feebleness with which we have acted since we helplessly drifted into the war—if these men now repented of the cruel wrong they have done this nation and mankind, we could afford to wrap their past folly and evil-doing in the kindly mantle of oblivion.

But they boast of their foolishness, they excuse and justify it, they announce that they feel pride and delight in contemplating it. Therefore it was for us, the people, to bow our heads on our penitential day; for we were laggards in the battle, we let others fight in our quarrel, we let others pay with their shattered bodies for the fire in their burning souls.

The trumpets of the Lord sounded for Armageddon, but our hearts were not swift to answer nor our feet jubilant; coldly we at home watched others die that we might live. Our rulers were supple and adroit; but they were not mighty of soul. They showed that they would not lead us, and would even stand in front only if we forced them forward.

Overseas our fighting men, by their valor and their suffering, are now atoning for the manifold failures in the past of our rulers at home. Now at last we can hold our heads aloft, because these, our sons and brothers, have won immortal honor, and have established records of efficient and heroic valor which give our nation the same right which the Allied nations already had to cherish forever sorrowful but glorious memories of this world war. But it behooves us to see that other millions of our fighting men stand beside them, and that they have every weapon and war machine necessary to enable them to win the war with the least expenditure of their gallant blood. Spilt milk in the past has meant spilt blood in the present. Spilt milk in the present will mean more spilt blood in the future.

This is the reason why we, the American people, must search our own hearts and with unflinching will insist that from now on not a day, not an hour shall be wasted until our giant but soft and lazy strength is hardened, until we ourselves take the burden from the shoulders of others, until we pay whatever price our past shortcomings demand, and with heads uplifted and spirit undaunted stride forward to the great goal of the peace of victorious right.

APPENDIX A

ACKNOWLEDGMENT

Most, but not all, of the material herein contained has appeared during the present year in the *Metropolitan Magazine*, in the Kansas City *Star*, in the Philadelphia *North American*, in the New York *Tribune*, and in certain speeches.

Four years ago, in the articles which soon afterward were gathered into book form under the title of "America and the World War," I wrote:

The great danger to peace, so far as this country is concerned, arises from such pacifists as those who have made and applauded our recent all-inclusive arbitration treaties. . . . These persons may succeed in impressing foreign nations with the belief that they represent our people . . . (if so, there will follow) long-drawn war. . . . It is those among us who would go to the front in such event—as . . . my four sons would go—who are the really far-sighted and earnest friends of peace. We desire measures taken in the real interest of peace, because we who at need would fight, but who earnestly hope never to be forced to fight, have most at stake in keeping peace. . . . In such a war the prime fact to be remembered is that the men really responsible for it would not be those who would pay the penalty. The ultrapacifists are rarely men who go to battle. Their fault or their folly would be expiated by the blood of countless thousands of plain and decent American citizens.

Events have made good precisely what I thus wrote. The leading pacifists of four years ago, and their sons and sons-in-law, are rarely to be found in the fighting line at the front. It is the men who then advocated preparedness who now pay for the failure to prepare and for the folly of some of our leaders, and the political unscrupulousness of others.

APPENDIX B

DISPOSITION OF THE NOBEL PEACE PRIZE FUND

August 22nd, 1918.

My dear Congressman Gallivan:

In accordance with the terms of the Congressional resolution introduced by you, in the House of Representatives, and by Senator Johnson, acting for Senator Williams, in the Senate, Secretary Redfield for the Commission returned to me the Nobel Peace Prize Fund. The securities when sold, plus the cash in hand, amounted to $45,482.83. I have disposed of this sum as follows:

To the American Red Cross, through the Treasurer, Mr. John Skelton Williams...........$6,900.00

The American Red Cross, and possibly some other war charities or war activities will receive further sums of money from my royalties on certain scenarios of motion pictures to be shortly produced by the McClure Company; all the royalties I receive from the pictures in question during the period of the war will be thus used.

To Mrs. Theodore Roosevelt, Jr., now working in the Y. M. C. A. in France................ 5,000.00

As Mrs. Roosevelt is working in the Y. M. C. A.

I suppose that some or most of the money will be used in connection therewith; but the disposal is absolutely at her discretion.

To the Young Men's Christian Association National War Work Council, through the treasurer, Mr. Cleveland H. Dodge.............. 4,000.00

To the Knights of Columbus War Activities Committee, through the treasurer, Mr. William J. Mulligan.......................... 4,000.00

To the Jewish Welfare Board, for War Activities, through the treasurer, Mr. Walter E. Sachs.. 4,000.00

To the Salvation Army War Fund, treasurer Mr. G. S. Reinhardsen 4,000.00
I have sent this check through Major Atkins, who has been doing admirable work in the battalion of the 26th Infantry in which my sons Theodore Jr. and Archibald have been serving.

To the Young Women's Christian Association War Work Council, Colored, through Mrs. Henry P. Davison 4,000.00
I have asked that Miss Eva Bolles be consulted in the disbursal of this item. My wife and I were very much struck with the work of Miss Bolles in connection with the Colored Hostess House at Camp Upton; and I have requested that the money be used for the hostess houses for colored troops and in work among colored women and girls in and about the camps and cantonments.

To Miss Emily Tyler Carow, at Porto Maurizo,
Italy, for work in connection with the Italian
Red Cross.................................... 1,000.00

> I send this sum merely as a token of my ad-
> miration of the high gallantry and efficiency
> of Italy's action.

To Langdon Warner, acting American Vice-
Consul at Harbin and Vladivostock, for the
Czecho-Slovaks, the extraordinary nature of
whose great and heroic feat is literally unparal-
leled, so far as I know in ancient or modern
warfare 1,000.00

> In this case, as in all the cases that follow, the
> value of the money contribution amounts
> to so little that it seems hardly worth send-
> ing; but the money was given to me by the
> Nobel Peace Prize Committee for my action
> in connection with the Peace of Portsmouth,
> which closed the Russo-Japanese War; and
> I wish to use it in part to show my admira-
> tion for the high heroism of the peoples who
> have done most and suffered most in this
> great war to secure liberty for all those na-
> tions, big or little, which lead self-respecting
> and orderly lives, and act justly and fairly
> by others.

To Madame Major Botchkareva, for use as she
deems wise, as a token of my respect for those
Russians who have refused to follow the Bolshevists in their betrayal to Germany of Russia, of the Allies, and of the cause of liberty
throughout the world...................... 1,000.00

To Herbert C. Hoover, for use in Belgium...... 1,000.00

To the Belgian Minister, for use among the Belgian refugees in Holland.................... 1,000.00

   In Holland the burden of caring for the Belgian victims of the German horror has been very heavy; I suggest, but do not direct, that the money be expended through the committee to which Miss Van der Flier belongs.

To the Servian Minister, for the Servian sufferers 1,000.00

To Paul Shimmon for use among the Armenians and Assyrian Christians..................... 1,000.00

   I send this through Mr. Shimmon because so far as I know he has never sought to excuse or justify what I regard as our inexcusable dereliction in duty in having failed to declare war on Turkey, and therefore in having failed to play a manly part in the effort permanently to remedy the hideous wrongs of the subjects of the Turk in the only really effective way, by destroying Turkish rule.

To M. L. Mirman, Prefect of Meurthe-et-Moselle, the lamentable sufferings of the people of whose prefecture happen to have been brought intimately before us...................... 500.00

To Mrs. Mary Cadwalader Jones, for further similar work in France 500.00

To Count Ishii, the Japanese Ambassador, for the Japanese Red Cross 500.00

   The Japanese Red Cross, like the American Red Cross, has raised large sums of money for use in the Allied countries; I send this merely as a very slight token of my admiration for the part the Japanese people have taken in this war.

To Leslie M. Tarlton, Nairobi, for any war activity, or war charity in Uganda or British East Africa.................................. 500.00

I was in Africa with Mr. Tarlton, who is an Australian. I send this merely as a token of my admiration of what has been done in this war by the Canadians, Australians, New Zealanders and Africanders, both of Boer and British blood.

To Mrs. Stewart Jobson for reconstruction work for wounded soldiers in England............. 500.00

To Judge Joseph L. Nunan, of Georgetown, Demerara, for wounded soldiers and their families in Ireland.......................... 500.00

I send this through Mr. Nunan because he believes in Home Rule within the Empire, and stands uncompromisingly for prosecuting the war against Germany with all possible efficiency until the enemy is completely overthrown.

To Henry P. Davison, to be used when possible for the Roumanians....................... 500.00

To Henry P. Davison, to be used when possible for the Montenegrins...................... 500.00

To Robert M. Thompson, for the Comforts Committee of the Navy League................. 500.00

To Speaker Champ Clark, for war activities or
    charities.................................... 500.00
    I suggest but do not stipulate that this be used
    in Missouri.

To Mrs. James A. Gallivan, for war activities
    or charities.............................. 500.00
    I suggest but do not stipulate that this be
    used in Mrs. Gallivan's own neighborhood
    in Massachusetts.

To Mrs. John A. Williams, for similar use...... 500.00
    I suggest but do not stipulate that this be
    used in Mississippi.

To Mrs. Hiram Johnson for similar use........ 500.000
    I suggest but do not stipulate that this be
    used in California.

For cabling and other expenses in connection
    therewith................................. 82.83
                              ————
        Total.............................$45,482.83

I wish to express my obligations to Secretary
Redfield and his associates for the promptness with
which they acted.

                Faithfully yours,
                    THEODORE ROOSEVELT.

HON. JAMES A. GALLIVAN,
    House of Representatives,
        Washington, D. C.

APPENDIX C

PUT THE BLAME WHERE IT BELONGS

Under the above heading I wrote to Senator Poindexter concerning the misconduct of the administration—especially through the action of Messrs. Burleson and Creel, and the handling of the Department of Justice and the War Department—in failing to act efficiently against German spies and pro-German traitors here at home, and in failing to proceed against powerful newspapers which supported Mr. Wilson personally although conducting an anti-ally or anti-war, and therefore anti-American and pro-German propaganda, while mercilessly interfering with the freedom of speech and with the freedom of the press as regards non-seditious and loyal papers which were politically opposed to the administration and which the administration desired to browbeat. This letter was put into the record by Senator Poindexter and has been reproduced as an appendix in Mr. James A. B. Scherer's admirable volume entitled "The Nation at War."

I showed that the great and powerful Hearst newspapers had been left unmolested by the administration (by administration I mean President Wilson and those intimate high subordinates and advisers of his who are his especial agents and for whose acts he must accept full responsibility), and had been helped by the administration through action which was not merely of political but of financial consequence to them; whereas weak papers and papers to which the administration objected on political grounds had been bullied and interfered with and even practically suppressed. I gave the facts in these and other cases in detail; and the administration never ventured to question these facts—because the members of the administration well knew that I was telling the absolute truth, and that no one could truthfully or successfully dispute what I had said.

The simple truth is that never in our history has any other administration during a great war played politics of the narrowest personal and partisan type as President Wilson has done; and one of the features of this effort has been the careful and studied effort to mislead and misinform the public through information sedulously and copiously furnished them by government officials. An even worse feature has been the largely successful effort to break down freedom of speech and the freedom of the press by government action. Much of this action has been taken under the guise of attacking disloyalty; but it has represented action, not against those who were disloyal to the nation, but against those who disagreed with or criticised the President for failure in the performance of duty to the nation. The action of the government against real traitors, and against German spies and agents, has been singularly weak and ineffective. The chief of the Secret Service said that there were a quarter of a million German spies in this country. Senator Overmann put the number at a larger figure; but not one has been shot or hung, and relatively few have been interfered with in any way. The real vigor of the administration has been directed against honest critics who have endeavored to force it to speed up the war and to act with prompt efficiency against Germany.

In my letter to Senator Poindexter I quoted an article I had written which appeared in the *Metropolitan Magazine* for April, 1918. It runs as follows:

LINCOLN AND FREE SPEECH

Patriotism means to stand by the country. It does not mean to stand by the President or any other public official save exactly to the degree in which he himself stands by the country. It is patriotic to support him in so far as he efficiently serves the country. It is unpatriotic not to oppose him to the exact extent that by inefficiency or otherwise he fails in his duty to stand by the country. In either event, it is unpatriotic not to tell the truth— whether about the President or about any one else—save in the rare cases where this would make known to the enemy information of military value which would otherwise be unknown to him.

Sedition, in the legal sense, means to betray the government, to give aid and comfort to the enemy, or to counsel resistance to the laws or to measures of government having the force of law. There can be conduct morally as bad as legal sedition which yet may not be violation of law. The President—any President—can by speech or action (by advocating an improper peace or improper submission to national wrong) give aid and comfort to the public enemy as no one else in the land can do, and yet his conduct, however damaging to the country, is not seditious; and although if public sentiment is sufficiently aroused he can be impeached, such course is practically impossible.

One form of servility consists in a slavish attitude—of the kind incompatible with self-respecting manliness—toward any person who is powerful by reason of his office or position. Servility may be shown by a public servant toward the profiteering head of a large corporation, or toward the anti-American head of a big labor organization. It may also be shown in peculiarly noxious and un-American form by confounding the President or any other official with the country and shrieking "stand by the President," without regard to whether, by so acting, we do or do not stand by the country.

A distinguished Federal judge recently wrote me as follows:

"Last November it seemed as if the American people were going to be converted into a hallelujah chorus, whose only function in government should be to shout 'Hallelujah!' 'Hallelujah!' for everything that the Administration did or failed to do. Any one who did not join that chorus was liable to imprisonment for treason or sedition.

"I hope that we shall soon have recovered our sense as well as our liberty.

"The authors of the first amendment to the Federal Constitution guaranteeing the right of assembly and of freedom of speech and of the press did not thus safeguard those rights for the sake alone of persons who were to enjoy them, but even more because they knew that the Republic which they were founding could not be worked on any other basis. Since Marshall tried Burr for treason it has been clear that that crime cannot be committed by words, unless one acts as a spy, or gives advice to the enemy of military or naval operations. It cannot be committed by statements reflecting upon officers or measures of government.

"Sedition is different. Any one who directly advises or counsels resistance to measures of government is guilty of sedition. That, however, ought to be clearly distinguished from discussion of the wisdom or folly of measures of government, or the honesty or competency of public officers. That is not sedition. It is within the protection of the first amendment. The electorate cannot be qualified to perform its duty in removing incompetent officers and securing the repeal of unwise laws unless those questions may be freely discussed.

"The right to say wise things necessarily implies the right to say foolish things. The answer to foolish speech is wise speech and not force. The Republic is founded upon the faith that if the American people are permitted freely to hear foolish and wise speech, a majority will choose the wise. If that faith is not justified the Republic is based on sand. John Milton said it all in his defense of freedom of the press: 'Let truth and error grapple. Who ever knew truth to be beaten in a fair fight?'"

Abraham Lincoln was in Congress while Polk was President, during the Mexican War. The following extracts from his speeches, during war-time, about the then President ought to be illuminating to those persons who do not understand that one of the highest and most patriotic duties to be performed in his country at this time is to tell the truth whenever it becomes necessary in order to force our government to speed up the war. It would, for example, be our highest duty to tell it if at any time we became convinced that only thereby could we shame our leaders out of hypocrisy and prevent the betrayal of human rights by peace talk of the kind which bewilders and deceives plain people.

These quotations can be found on pages 100 to 146 of volume I of "Lincoln's Complete Works," by Nicolay and Hay.

In a speech on January 12, 1848, Lincoln justified himself for voting in favor of a resolution censuring the President for his action prior to and during the war (which was still going on). He examines the President's official message of justification and says, "that, taking for true all the President states as facts, he falls far short of proving his justification, and that the President would have gone further with his proof if it had not been for the small matter that the truth would not permit him." He says that part of the message "is from beginning to end the sheerest deception." He then asks the President to answer certain questions, and says, "Let him answer fully, fairly, and candidly. Let him answer with facts and not with arguments. Let him remember that he sits where Washington sat, and so remembering, let him answer as Washington would answer. Let him attempt no evasion, no equivocation." In other words, Lincoln says that he does not wish rhetoric or fine phrases or glittering statements that contradict one another and each of which has to be explained with a separate key or adroit and subtle special pleading and constant reversal of positions previously held, but straightforward and consistent adherence to the truth. He continues that he "more than suspects" that the President "is deeply conscious of being in the wrong; that he feels that" innocent blood "is crying to heaven against him"; that one of the best generals had "been driven into disfavor, if not disgrace, by the President" for insisting upon speaking unpalatable truths

about the length of time the war would take (and therefore the need of full preparedness); and ends by saying
that the army has done admirably, but that the President
has bungled his work and "knows not where he is. He
is a bewildered, confounded, and miserably perplexed
man. God grant he may be able to show there is not something about his conscience more painful than all his mental perplexity."

Remember that this is Lincoln speaking, in war-time,
of the President. The general verdict of history has justified him. But it is impossible to justify him and not
heartily to condemn the persons who in our time endeavor
to suppress truth telling of a far less emphatic type than
Lincoln's.

Lincoln had to deal with various critics of the "stand
by the President" type. To one he answers that "the
only alternative is to tell the truth or to lie," and that
he would not "skulk" on such a question. He explains
that the President's supporters "are untiring in their
efforts to make the impression that all who vote supplies
or take part in the war do of necessity approve the President's conduct," but that he (Lincoln) and his associates
sharply distinguished between the two and voted supplies
and men but "denounced the President's conduct" and
"condemned the administration." He stated that to give
the President the power demanded for him by certain people would "place the President where kings have always
stood." In touching on what we should now speak of as
rhetoric, he says, "The honest laborer digs coal at about
seventy cents a day, while the President digs abstractions at about seventy dollars a day. The coal is clearly
worth more than the abstractions, and yet what a mon-
strous inequality in the price!" He emphatically protests
against permitting the President "to take the whole of
legislation into his hands"—surely a statement applying
exactly to the present situation. To the President's servile

party supporters he makes a distinction which also readily applies at the present day, "The distinction between the cause of the President . . . and the cause of the country . . . you cannot perceive. To you the President and the country seem to be all one. . . . We see the distinction clearly enough."

This last statement was the crux of the matter then and is the crux of the matter now. We hold that our loyalty is due solely to the American Republic, and to all our public servants exactly in proportion as they efficiently and faithfully serve the Republic. Our opponents, in flat contradiction of Lincoln's position, hold that our loyalty is due to the President, not the country; to one man, the servant of the people, instead of to the people themselves. In practice they adopt the fetishism of all believers in absolutism, for every man who parrots the cry of "stand by the President" without adding the proviso "so far as he serves the Republic" takes an attitude as essentially unmanly as that of any Stuart royalist who championed the doctrine that the king could do no wrong. No self-respecting and intelligent freeman can take such an attitude.

The Wisconsin Legislature has just set forth the proper American doctrine, as follows:

"The people of the State of Wisconsin always have stood and always will stand squarely behind the National Government in all things which are essential to bring the present war to a successful end, and we condemn Senator Robert La Follette and all others who have failed to see the righteousness of our Nation's cause, who have failed to support our Government in matters vital to the winning of the war, and we denounce any attitude or utterance of theirs which has tended to incite sedition among the people of our country."

In view of the recent attitude of the administration as expressed through the Attorney-General and Postmaster-

General I commend to its attention the utterances of Abraham Lincoln in 1848 and of the Wisconsin Legislature in 1918. The administration's warfare against German spies and American traitors has been feeble. The government has achieved far less in this direction than has been achieved by a few of our newspapers and by various private individuals. This failure is aggravated by such action as was threatened against the *Metropolitan Magazine*. The *Metropolitan*—and the present writer—have stood and will continue to stand, "squarely behind the National Government in all things which are essential to bring the present war to a successful end" and to support "the righteousness of the Nation's cause." We will stand behind the country at every point, and we will at every point either support or oppose the administration precisely in proportion as it does or does not with efficiency and single-minded devotion serve the country.

From this position we will not be driven by any abuse of power or by any effort to make us not the loyal servants of the American people, but the cringing tools of a man who at the moment has power.

The administration has in some of its actions on vital points shown great inefficiency (as proved by Senator Chamberlain's committee) and on other points has been guilty of conduct toward certain peoples wholly inconsistent with its conduct toward other peoples and wholly inconsistent with its public professions as regards all international conduct. It cannot meet these accusations, for they are truthful, and to try to suppress the truth by preventing the circulation of the *Metropolitan Magazine* is as high-handed a defiance of liberty and justice as anything done by the Hohenzollerns or the Romanoffs. Such action is intolerable. Contrast the leniency shown by the government toward the grossest offenses against the nation with its eagerness to assail any one who tells

unpleasant truths about the administration. The Hearst
papers play the German game when they oppose the war,
assail our Allies, and clamor for an inconclusive peace,
and they play the German game when they assail the men
who truthfully point out the shortcomings which, unless
corrected, will redound to Germany's advantage and
our terrible disadvantage. But the administration has
taken no action against the Hearst papers. The *Metropolitan Magazine* has supported the war, has championed
every measure to speed up the war and to make our
strength effective, and has stood against every proposal
for a peace without victory. But the administration acts
against the magazine that in straightforward American
fashion has championed the war. Such discrimination
is not compatible with either honesty or patriotism. It
means that the administration is using the great power
of the government to punish honest criticism of its shortcomings, while it accepts support of and apology for these
shortcomings as an offset to action against the war and,
therefore, against the nation. Conduct of this kind is
a grave abuse of official power.

Whatever the administration does, I shall continue
to act in the future precisely as I have acted in the past.
When a senator like Mr. Chamberlain in some great
matter serves the country better than does the administration, I shall support that senator; and when a senator
like Mr. La Follette perseveres in the course followed by
the administration before it reversed itself in February,
1917, I shall oppose him and to that extent support the
administration in its present position. I shall continue
to support the administration in every such action as
floating the liberty loans, raising the draft army, or sending our troops abroad. I shall continue truthfully to
criticise any flagrant acts of incompetency by the administration, such as the failure in shipping matters and
the breakdown of the War Department during the last

fourteen months, when it appears that such truthful criticism offers the only chance of remedying the wrong. I shall support every official from the President down who does well, and shall oppose every such official who does ill. I shall not put the personal comfort of the President or of any other public servant above the welfare of the country.

I contemptuously refuse to recognize any American adaptation of the German doctrine of lese-majesty. I am concerned only with the welfare of my beloved country and with the effort to beat down the German horror in the interest of the orderly freedom of all the nations of mankind. If the administration does the work of war with all possible speed and efficiency, and stands for preparedness as a permanent policy, and heartily supports our allies to the end, and insists upon complete victory as a basis for peace, I shall heartily support it. If the administration moves in the direction of an improper peace, of the peace of defeat and of cowardice, or if it wages war feebly and timidly, I shall oppose it and shall endeavor to wake the American people to their danger.

I hold that only in this way can I act as patriotism bids me act. I hold that only in this way can I serve in even the slightest degree the cause of America, of the Allies, and of liberty; and that only thus can I aid in thwarting Germany's effort to establish a world tyranny.

APPENDIX D

THE TERMS OF PEACE

ADDRESS AT LAFAYETTE DAY EXERCISES, ALDER-
MANIC CHAMBERS, NEW YORK CITY, SEPTEMBER
6TH, 1918, BY THEODORE ROOSEVELT

Lafayette Day commemorates the services rendered to America in the Revolution by France. I
wish to insist with all possible emphasis that in the
present war France and England and Italy and the
other Allies have rendered us similar services. The
French at the battle of the Marne four years ago,
and at Verdun, and the British at Ypres—in short,
the French, the English, the Italians, the Belgians,
the Serbians have been fighting for us when they
were fighting for themselves. Our army on the
other side is now repaying in part our debt, and
next year we have every reason to hope, and we
must insist, that the fighting army in France from
the United States shall surpass in numbers the
fighting army in France, of either France or England. It is now time—and it long has been time
—for America to bear her full share of the common
burden, the burden borne by all the Allies in this
great war for liberty and justice.

We must win the war as speedily as possible.

But we must set ourselves to fight it through no matter how long it takes, with the resolute determination to accept no peace until, no matter at what cost, we win the peace of overwhelming victory. The peace that we win must guarantee full reparation for the awful cost of life and treasure which the Prussianized Germany of the Hohenzollerns has inflicted on the entire world; and this reparation must take the form of action that will render it impossible for Germany to repeat her colossal wrong-doing. Germany has been able to wage this fight for world dominion because she has subdued to her purpose her vassal allies, Austria, Turkey, and Bulgaria. Serbia and Roumania must have restored to them what Bulgaria has taken from them. The Austrian and Turkish Empires must both be broken up, all the subject peoples liberated, and the Turk driven from Europe. We do not intend that German or Magyar shall be oppressed by others, but neither do we intend that they shall oppress and domineer over others. France must receive back Alsace and Lorraine. Belgium must be restored and indemnified. Italian Austria must be restored to Italy, and Roumanian Hungary to Roumania. The heroic Czech-Slovaks must be made into an independent commonwealth. The southern Slavs must be united in a great Jugo-Slav commonwealth. Poland as a genuinely independent commonwealth must receive back Austrian and Prussian Poland, as well as Russian Poland, and have her

coast line on the Baltic. Lithuania, the Baltic
Provinces of Russia, Ukrania, and Finland must be
guaranteed their independence, and no part of the
ancient empire of Russia left under the German
yoke, or subject in any way to German influence.
Northern Schleswig should go back to the Danes.
Britain and Japan should keep the colonies they
have conquered. Armenia must be freed, Palestine
made a Jewish state, the Greeks guaranteed their
rights, and the Syrians liberated—all of them, Mo-
hammedans, Jews, Druses, and Christians, being
guaranteed an equal liberty of religious belief, and
required to work out their independence on the
basis of equal political and civil rights for all
creeds.

It is sometimes announced that part of the peace
agreement must be a League of Nations, which will
avert all war for the future, and put a stop to the
need of this nation preparing its own strength for
its own defense. Many of the adherents of this
idea grandiloquently assert that they intend to
supplant nationalism by internationalism.

In deciding upon proposals of this nature it behooves our people to remember that competitive
rhetoric is a poor substitute for the habit of resolutely looking facts in the face. Nothing in the
world can alter facts. Patriotism stands in national matters as love of family does in private life.
Nationalism corresponds to the love a man bears
for his wife and children. Internationalism corre-

sponds to the feeling he has for his neighbors generally. The sound nationalist is the only type of really helpful internationalist, precisely as in private relations it is the man who is most devoted to his own wife and children who is apt, in the long run, to be the most satisfactory neighbor. To substitute internationalism for nationalism means to do away with patriotism, and is as vicious and as profoundly demoralizing as to put promiscuous devotion to all other persons in the place of steadfast devotion to a man's own family. Either effort means the atrophy of robust morality. The man who loves other countries as much as his own stands on a level with the man who loves other women as much as he loves his own wife. One is as worthless a creature as the other. The professional pacifist and the professional internationalist are equally undesirable citizens. The American pacifist has in actual fact shown himself to be the tool and ally of the German militarist. The professional internationalist is a man who, under a pretense of diffuse attachment for everybody hides the fact that in reality he is incapable of doing his duty by anybody.

We Americans should abhor all wrong-doing to other nations. We ought always to act fairly and generously by other nations. But we must remember that our first duty is to be loyal and patriotic citizens of our own nation, of America. These two facts should always be in our minds in dealing with any proposal for a League of Nations. By all means let us be loyal to great ideals. But let us remember that, unless we show common sense in action, loyalty in speech will amount to considerably less than nothing.

Test the proposed future League of Nations so far as concerns proposals to disarm, and to trust to anything except our own strength for our own defense, by what the nations are actually doing at the present time. Any such league would have to depend for its success upon the adhesion of the nine nations which are actually or potentially the most powerful military nations, and these nine nations include Germany, Austria, Turkey, and Russia. The first three have recently and repeatedly violated, and are now actively and continuously violating, not only every treaty, but every rule of civilized warfare and of international good faith. During the last year Russia, under the dominion of the Bolshevists, has betrayed her allies, has become the tool of the German autocracy, and has shown such utter disregard of her national honor and plighted word, and her international duties, that she is now in external affairs the passive tool and ally of her brutal conqueror, Germany. What earthly use is it to pretend that the safety of the world would be secured by a League in which these four nations would be among the nine leading partners? Long years must pass before we can again trust any promises these four nations make. Any treaty of any kind or sort which we make with them should be made with the full understanding that they will cynically repudiate it whenever they think it to their interest to do so. Therefore, unless our folly is such that it will not depart from us until we are brayed in a mortar, let us remember that any such treaty will be worthless unless our own prepared strength renders it unsafe to break it.

After the war the wrong-doers will be so punished and exhausted that they may for a number of years wish to keep the peace. But the surest way to make them keep the peace in the future is to punish them heavily now. And don't forget that China is now useless as a prop to a League of Peace, simply because she lacks effective military strength for her own defense.

Let us support any reasonable plan, whether in the form of a League of Nations or in any other shape, which bids fair to lessen the probable number of future wars, and to limit their scope.[1] But let us laugh out of court any assertion that any such plan will guarantee peace and safety to the foolish, weak

[1] In my book already alluded to, published nearly four years ago under the title "America and the World War," there will be found what so far as I know is the most feasible plan for actually putting into effect such a League of Nations to enforce peace. What I therein wrote on the subject is sound doctrine to-day; and if what I therein wrote (in October, November, and December, 1914) as to performing our international duty, and as to preparedness, had been acted upon by the administration at Washington, this war would long have been over, we would now have the peace of right and justice, and incalculable bloodshed would have been saved.

or timid creatures who have not the will and the power to prepare for their own defense. Support any such plan which is honest and reasonable. But support it as an addition to, and never as a substitute for, the policy of preparing our own strength for our own defense. To follow any other course would turn this country into the China of the Occident. We cannot guarantee for ourselves or our children peace without effort, or safety without service and sacrifice. We must prepare both our souls and our bodies, in virile fashion, alike to secure justice for ourselves and to do justice to others. Only thus can we secure our own national self-respect. Only thus can we secure the respect of other nations and the power to aid them when they seek to do well.

In sum, then, I shall be delighted to support the movement for a League to Enforce Peace, or for a League of Nations, if it is developed as a supplement to, and not a substitute for, the preparation of our own strength. I believe that this preparation should be by the introduction in this country of the principle of universal training and universal service, as practised in Switzerland, and modified, of course, both along the lines indicated in Australia and in accordance with our own needs. There will be no taint of Prussian militarism in such a system. It will merely mean ability to fight for self-defense in a great democracy in which law, order, and liberty are to prevail.

APPENDIX E

STRAIGHT-OUT AMERICANISM

I cannot resist putting in the following letter, because it shows just what Americanism demands in the face of Germany at this time, and because it shows what a thoroughgoing American the average young American of German parentage or descent is—for the gallant young soldier who writes this letter is typical of the hundreds of thousands of other gallant young American soldiers, in whole or in part of German blood—and typical of all the millions of other young American soldiers, Protestant, Catholic, and Jew, of old native American stock, or of Irish, English, Scandinavian, Slavonic, French, Italian parentage.

The writer of the letter is Lieutenant Earl B. Mahle, a second lieutenant of a machine-gun company, who had been gassed in battle. The letter is written from a hospital, on July 20, 1918. It was addressed to his uncle, the Reverend W. E. Mahle, of Blooming Grove, Minnesota. It runs in part as follows:

In your letter you asked a lot of questions the like of which you say I have to answer when I get back. I see no objection in answering a few of them now.

You wonder how we feel when given the opportunity

197

to mow them down like grass as they advance. I know just what you are thinking when you ask that question. I used to think that I would have to reconstitute my ideals, allow them to descend to a lower plane, in order to derive any satisfaction from even killing the enemy in battle. Now I admire the man who asks the doctor to patch him up a bit so that he can go out and get a few more "boches" before they finish him. Why shouldn't we derive some satisfaction at being able to help do away with a breed that cannot deal honestly, but practices deception at every turn; a breed that delights in flying above a procession of innocent women and children refugees, and shooting them down like dogs with the aviator's machine-gun; that will swoop down upon a Red Cross hospital tent, and deliberately inflict wounds on those already terribly wounded, and deliberately shoot down those beautiful souls, the Red Cross nurses, as they minister to those who are suffering; that practices the bombing of hospitals, and uses its own Red Cross hospital tents as a camouflage for ammunition dumps; that after the battle is over, deliberately shoots down our Red Cross personnel as they make an attempt to bring help to the wounded; a breed that sees nothing sacred in womanhood, that has no religion but its own desires, and knows no law but its own passions. Really I do not think even the most exacting of persons could have any compunctions of conscience about shooting down the class of people we have as our enemy. I have a firm conviction that our nation has been divinely called or favored to show to Germany and her allies that they cannot continue in their criminal policy indefinitely without answering for all the suffering and devastation that has been caused. After seeing what I have I am firmly convinced that our dead will not have died in vain, that those Americans who have lost loved ones in this war should not mourn but should take satisfaction. The greater the sacrifice, the greater will be their reward.

I am glad to hear you say that America is loyal everywhere. It is the right and duty of every citizen to see to it that this loyalty is entire, that those persons who are found uttering pro-German or anti-ally sentiments are arrested and brought before our department of justice. No person should have any regrets about being able to render such a service to our cause.

But that brings me to think again about something that I have thought about a good deal lately. We have said a great deal about pro-Germanism. and have condemned it violently, but we have said comparatively little about the use of the German language, and what could be more pro-German than the German language, what could be more anti-American in these times? It is the official language of "Kaiserism," it is the agent by means of which it was sought to spread abroad even in our own fair land the much-despised German "Kultur."

We have taught the German language in our schools. We were told it was next in importance to English itself. Now we find it hard to explain why German was any more important to our American than French or Italian or Spanish. In our churches we used the German language in the practice of our religion, in many instances among people who were born in America and educated in its schools and who certainly could more readily understand the English language. No one can easily explain the reason for the last mentioned stubbornness.

Just before I left America some one suggested in my presence that we ought to bar the German language from a place in the course of study in our high schools. To this I objected. In our ardent patriotism we should be careful not to run off on a tangent, we should bear in mind the essentials and forget trivialities. Thus I argued. I had studied German, I could speak and even felt in a measure prepared to teach it. Was not the German language the language in which Goethe and Schiller expressed such noble truths and beautiful sentiments. There are

noble truths and beautiful sentiments given expression
in other languages too, but in their cases we use trans-
lations. May we still love Goethe and Schiller, but at
the same time realize that to-day their language is the
language of "Kaiserism" and "Kultur," which stands
for everything that is low and mean and deceitful. We
are living to-day, and must face conditions as they are
to-day. To-day, the average American with average information knows that it was part of a pre-conceived plan
of Kaiser Wilhelm and his band of Potsdam cut-throats
to have German taught in our schools, to have German
used in our churches, to have newspapers published in
the German language, which should exert an ever-in-
creasing influence upon millions of people in America, of
German descent, who in turn would by their vote have a
tremendous influence upon the political situations, gradually bringing about a turn of events highly favorable to
the propagation of German autocracy in America.

We are at war with Germany, with Germans who speak
as their language the German language. It can no longer
be said of our troops that "they are going and will soon
give an account of themselves." They are already here.
They have shown on numerous occasions that they have
the true American spirit. They have never yet been de-
feated, no, not even by superior numbers. (I say this
with some degree of pride and I know it is pardonable.)
But to-day the American army does not consist alone
of the men who are in France. Every American man,
woman, and child whether in America or abroad is a soldier
in our army. We have all enlisted. Those at home must
be just as much 100-per-cent Americans as those keeping
eternal vigilance in the dead of night at the edge of No
Man's Land. The man who has lived in America and
still enjoys its advantages and promises, and can speak
only the German language, is not a 100-per-cent American.
He does not and will not comprehend our American ideals
and standards.

He bears watching. The man who prefers to speak German even though he can speak some English is an enemy of the United States. Every American knows what should be done with him. Do you imagine that we allow our soldiers to speak the German language among themselves. I have never yet seen where they wanted to do it, but if they did, would we be right in allowing it. If I were to hear two men in America conversing in the enemy tongue, it would be my business to find out "why."

America's men, the prime of her youth, are in France fighting for a principle. They are deprived of comfort, many are suffering and dying. Some of them will never again be able to return to the land of their youth and the land of promise; they gave all, and they gave it willingly. Some others will return even before the war is over. They will have given much, an arm, a limb or possibly their eyesight; and they will have given gladly and without complaint. You will receive them in America in a grand and beautiful way; no doubt you will make them feel that they are "heroes." But tell me, are these same men to return to hear spoken all about them the German language, are German newspapers to announce their return and comment on their wounds, are they going to be insulted in such a fashion? Are they to go to church and hear Christianity preached to them in an enemy tongue? Can you see how these boys could get a full measure of comfort out of a religion preached to them in the language of the enemy with whom they had been engaged in mortal combat, the enemy who violated every principle of that same religion which is Christianity? Tell me is there something essential to Christianity in the German language? Is it the language that makes Christianity or is it the spirit of Christ after all? Have we not heard about false gods somewhere, before this?

Yes, these are tremendous times. There was a time when we would have said of a man who so desired, that he was an American until he proved by his conduct that he was otherwise. To-day is different. To-day we do not accept mere statements. To-day no man is a loyal American until he has proved himself to be one. What I mean to say is that to-day there is no passive Americanism, to-day every loyal American must be an active American willing to co-operate in every way for the promotion of Americanism, ready to do all in his power to advance the cause for which we are struggling, and to suppress pro-Germanism and Pan-Germanism in whatever form it may appear.

When you go to the conference you will meet many with whom I am acquainted, probably many who have loved ones over here. Tell them for me that they shall be proud of their American soldiers, and even if there will be those who will not return, as there will be, they should not mourn but should have the same faith that their boys had, a faith in God, and in their cause, and an ever readiness to do the thing that was expected of them.

Almost at the same time that this letter was written the following letter, preaching the same fine and lofty Americanism, was written me by a Catholic chaplain serving with the army under General Pershing.

> With the Army in France,
> Dugout No.——, July 18, 1918.

DEAR COLONEL ROOSEVELT:

In the name of this Artillery Brigade, upon the heroic death of your son and our comrade, Lieut. Roosevelt, I extend to the family our heartfelt condolences. To you, Sir, I have the honor of offering our congratulations. He died the death of a soldier. You would not have it otherwise.

Your gallant son, who was one of the most dashing

officers in an arm of the Service well known for reckless bravery, has not died in vain. His death in the great cause for which we are fighting, will do more to convince the hideous Hun of the earnestness of our purpose, than the work of an Army Division. Be assured that his heroic death will not go unavenged. We shall see to it that the barbarian pays for it in measure heaped up and running over. It has already enthused the Army and strengthened our hands.

Through you, may I send a message to the folks back home—particularly to my people of Irish lineage and the Catholics of America. If amongst them there remains a single individual obstinately "unconverted" to the righteousness of the cause for which we are here under the guns, that man is a traitor and should be dealt with accordingly. I am speaking as a priest of the Catholic Church when I say that I believe every one of our countrymen should develop a healthy hatred for the unregenerate German, and for everything that smacks of thrice-accursed German Kultur.

I beg leave to send this message through you, because you were always just and fair to our Catholic people and they regard you as their friend. I am weighing my words, and can prove them when I say that nearly fifty per cent of the Army under fire to day is Catholic. England-baiters back home are doing their best to destroy the record that we are building. They deserve no quarter.

You have been friendly to the Jew as well as to the Catholic. You may be interested therefore to know that many of our best officers and men are Jews. Among them I have the stanchest friends. As a Catholic priest, I take my hat off to the Jew for heroism on the field of battle and loyalty at home.

Here too let me say a word for the Y. M. C. A. When the history of this great war is written, the historian will in justice be obliged to give not a little of the glory of victory to the courage, self-sacrifice, and efficiency of the men who wore the red triangle. I say to you, Sir, it is an inspiring sight to see the spirit of real fraternity there is among the troops in the field—Catholic and Protestant and Jew standing as one man presenting a solid front to a common enemy. And I believe, as I believe there is a God above, that one of the important by-products of this war is going to be a better spirit of mutual understanding and toleration all around. The war is going to weld the country together as it never was welded before. The spirit of the men here is that we are going to win the war, though it cost the last dollar and the last man. We are counting on the same spirit at home and I believe that we are not going to be disappointed.

Kindly pardon my undignified longhand script. A typewriting-machine is too great a luxury in this cave 40 feet underground. Dugout No.— is not the most comfortable office-room in the world. My mahogany desk is a pile of empty cartridge-boxes that threatens to topple over very time the earth quakes on the booming of our guns—which is almost continually. We all wear rubber boots and are splashed over with yellow mud and refreshing ice cold spring-water. We sleep in our gas-masks. I have occupied more comfortable quarters, yet withal, I am very happy here. It is an excellent vantage-point from which to view and study Hunnish ruthlessness. If a Chaplain could be pardoned for quasi-profanity, I would say with all my heart: "Anathema sit to the accursed Hun and everything connected with his accursed scheme of world conquest."

Very truly yours,
VINCENT J. TOOLE,
Chaplain 324 Field Artillery.

Date Due

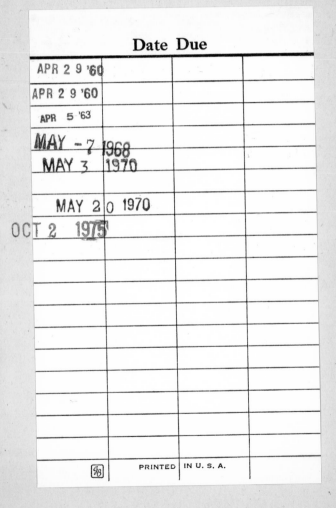